GIRLFRIENDS 2.0

Cindy W Morrison

Girlfriends 2.0: Reboot and Upgrade Your Girlfriends NOW!
ISBN: 978-1-936750-03-0
Copyright © 2010 by Cindy W Morrison

Published by
Yorkshire Publishing
9731 East 54th Street
Tulsa, OK 74146
www.yorkshirepublishing.com

Dedication

This book is dedicated to
my young precious daughter, Marlowe.

I can't wait to share many Girlfriend moments as
you grow, and I hope you'll use this as a guide to
surround yourself by only the best peeps possible.
Your MiMi (my Mom) is my original Girlfriend,
and I look forward to that same special bond
with you!

(Ladies, we must continue to pass along our
best ideas and encourage the next generation
to be Girlfriend-worthy.)

Forward

We connected as many people do these days — on the web, specifically Twitter — when she began showing up to say extremely nice things about my workplace segments on ABC's Good Morning America.

She caught my attention immediately: what woman doesn't enjoy praise? But Cindy didn't stop there: being generous and smart, she always managed to suggest ideas for future segments, without asking anything in return.

I'll admit that I didn't run with every one her ideas, but a few of them really clicked. I quickly began to pay attention whenever Cindy's name popped up on my screen.

When I found out that she and I both shared the unlikely experience of being booted from dream jobs in TV news (I was a young publicist, she an award-winning local anchor) I knew I had to get to know her. And over the next few months we did just that.

In August 2010 in Atlanta, when I kicked off my first Spark & Hustle conference for current and aspiring women entrepreneurs, I invited Cindy to speak on the opening day.

She wowed 200 women in the audience with her engaging story of her own personal reinvention. Of how, just as she was riding the TV news crest in Tulsa, Okla., confident in her journalism abilities, secure professionally and having a blast, her life suddenly came crashing down a la Broadcast News, her bosses informed her that her contract was not being renewed.

She was out.

How many millions of people across the country can relate to that these days? I can — fired without warning from NBC News in New York, something that scars me to this day.

But as traumatizing as it was, it did not prevent me from dusting myself off and getting back up. And it didn't stop Cindy, either. Sure, she took some needed time to mourn the loss of her career – before coming to this smart conclusion: reinvention is truly the greatest journey that any of us can take.

She now teaches other women across the country how to reinvent their careers – to have a life that works for them.

Cindy has become one of my closest friends — we talk or email every day. I admire her for her integrity, wisdom, drive and determination. She's on the mission to help others — and I can't think of anyone I'd rather support. This is definitely one Girlfriend (with a capital G, as Cindy's phenomenal book has taught me) that every one of us should want on our side.

Tory Johnson
Good Morning America Workplace Contributor
SparkandHustle.com Founder

Endorsements

"Whether you're trying to save money, start a career or build a business, "Girlfriends 2.0" is savvy –sassy-- and an inspiration."

—Elisabeth Leamy, Consumer Correspondent ABCNews

"We met on Twitter and through our 140-character exchanges I've come to believe that all women need Cindy—and her advice—on their side. Her candor and confidence will help you through any challenge."

—Tory Johnson, Good Morning America Contributor

"Cindy's gorgeous girlfriend speak and her humongous heart make Girlfriends 2.0 a vital tool for your friendship tool-kit. It's a must read for those of you looking to reinvent your life and upgrade your relationships. But most of all it invites us to never give up on our passions and to cherish even deeper our true friends!"

—Jess Weiner, Author,
Self-Esteem Expert, Advice Columnist

"Girlfriends 2.0 delivers a refreshing philosophy on identifiable standards for friendship"

—Beth Anderson, Chic Galleria magazine

"Cindy's insight into true friendships and how they connect through the modern diva's successful life struck me as honest and inspiring. Every true diva needs to read Girlfriends 2.0 and take to heart the lessons on finding, keeping and cherishing the kinds of relationships that move us all forward in every way."

—Janet Powers, Chief Executive Diva,
Diva Toolbox™ LLC

"Very often girlfriends are the most valuable resources women have! Cindy Morrison teaches women how the power of friendship can strengthen us in every area of our lives. Run, don't walk, and buy her fabulous book 'Girlfriends 2.0'!"

—Paula Fellingham, CEO,
The Women's Information Network

Cindy is the epitome of beauty and brains, as well as dynamic and hysterical! She's a collaborator, not a competitor, and is on a mission to empower women by sharing her vast network of resources. Cindy is every girl's BFF, and this book will show you why.

—Kelly Breen
Editor of Women of Wisdom Magazine

"Cindy mastered the art of reinvention. She caught wind of a possible layoff and had a book, speaking career and consulting business up and running before her last day on the job. I knew the moment we met at a National Speakers Association meeting she was destined for great things. If you're looking for someone to empower you to use social media to your advantage, build a better support network or become prime time ready... then she's your gal!"

—Dr Jeff Magee,
Performance Magazine

"I just finished your *Girlfriends 2.0* book last night. What a great story--we should all have friends like that and it's a great example of women helping each other and not competing with each other. Those Sabotage Suzie's need to be humanized."

—Gail McMeekin,
Author of *The 12 Secrets of Highly Creative*

Table of Contents

On the set of the evening news

Honored with a Gracie Award

After winning an Emmy

Anchor pic

Preface

I'll never forget the words my news director said in January 2009 that would change my world forever, "We don't know if we can renew your contract. It depends on the economy."

What? I remember being numb. He can't mean *me*?! In my mind, I rationalized a lot of things:

1. I've done the five o'clock evening news here for almost twelve years and have won awards. (Just look...they're on my mantel.)

2. Most viewers love me! (Those are the only ones I choose to listen to anyway.)

3. I constantly work twenty years' worth of contacts in Oklahoma to bring our station exclusive stories. (That single word 'exclusive' usually brings goose bumps to any news director!)

4. I make more appearances than any other anchor here. (Well, that's mainly because I can't say "no," but it still counts.)

5. I even help mentor our young, green journalists. (Oh, God, have I trained my replacement?)

Deep down I knew, before I heard those words from my news director, things weren't all roses at the TV station where I worked. Viewership at stations across the country had declined during the last ten years or so. We have competition from all those dang cable stations and the Internet (which I call "Insta-net" news). Fewer TV viewers mean the stations make less advertising money to pay salaries and operating costs. Add the fact advertisers aren't spending as much because of the state of the current economy, and it's tough times in TV Newsland, let me tell you.

But honestly, I didn't think that affected me (see my rationalizations #1-5 above). In fact, the week before the somber meeting with my news director, I was having the most fab spending spree with two of my best Girlfriends in Vegas. One morning during that vacay, I got a call about a second round of layoffs at my station. More? How was that possible? That made a total of twenty-five people laid off from our Tulsa, Oklahoma station in a matter of three months. That was about a fourth or fifth of our staff! On top of that, the co-worker who called me in Vegas then told me there were "voluntary" pay cuts (gulp!), and the company would stop matching our 401ks (ouch!). But hey, I still felt semi-safe. I mean, I had a contract, right? (That's what I rationalized when I bought a new Jimmy Choo bag in Vegas on sale.) The problem with my mindset at the time was that I chose to overlook (read "ignore") that my contract was up in only five months (July 1, 2009). If the economy didn't get better, my twenty-year career in TV news would be over. Just like that. All the awards in the world couldn't save me.

Wow....

More on my very public lay-off and a few other surprises a bit later, but basically, I knew from that moment sitting in my news director's office that I had five months to reinvent myself. However, did I know how to be anything but a newscaster? I had majored in journalism, not business! Tragedy can strike and I can ad-lib from the news set with ease, or write an award-winning story that will rip your heart apart, but ask me to do a simple business plan (or simple math for that matter) and I get cold and clammy. Now I had to reinvent myself at *mid-life*? I wasn't sure I had the strength.

Luckily, over the next five months, my family and Girlfriends picked me up like Humpty Dumpty and put me back together again. (Unfortunately, there wasn't a darn plastic surgeon among them, but I digress.) Here's where my Girlfriends weren't some old 1.0 version who just helped me find a job. My 2.0 Girlfriends changed my mindset and helped me to not only survive, but to thrive! You see, before the meeting with my news director, my life was like a current television ad running for AT&T. In the commercial, people are walking in a field (a herd of sheep, basically) saying "bah bah bah," when two guys decide to jump the fence and take the better deal with AT&T. I totally identified with that commercial because that was me! I was happy being a sheep, getting my paycheck, and staying with the herd (bah...!). Well, when my life suddenly changed because of the economy, it was my 2.0 Girlfriends who showed me it's okay to find my new place outside the herd because, apparently, Corporate America is having lamb chops for dinner!

Does something in your life threaten to serve you up as the next meal? Is there a fence you need to jump? Don't wait. You may not be able to pick your parents, you may or may not have picked your spouse very well, but you can pick wonderful and supportive Girlfriends right now. This is a book about rebooting, upgrading, and building a support group so you can survive, and even thrive, anything difficult that comes your way in this changing time—a death, a divorce, and even a very public lay-off.

Nine Bridesmaids (from lower left clockwise) Cindy, Janna,
Mignon, Julie B, Julie K, Rhonda, Kristy, Teresa & Sheila

Our December 1991 Wedding

CHAPTER 1

Nine Bridesmaids?!

Yes, I know what you are thinking: nine bridesmaids is a bit over the top (you'll soon learn I don't do anything halfway). But the truth is that once I learned the value of a really good Girlfriend, I managed to pick up at least one in every facet of my life. And when I tell you the precious gift each one of these girls gave me as I embarked on a new stage of my life, you'll understand why I had to have each one there when I said "I do." These nine Girlfriends helped me raise the bar on who I let into my "inner circle" from then on. True Girlfriends make such a difference in your life. Some of these girls I still see today, but all have a place in my heart, can call me tomorrow and I'll come running, and they definitely changed me forever.

Lubbock, TX

My first really close Girlfriend was Kristy from Monterey High School in Lubbock, Texas. You see, most of my friends before were boys. I was a tomboy until junior high when I began to cheer. I felt comfortable hanging with the boys. They didn't have high expectations, "play games," or say things they didn't mean (back then, anyway). Kristy and I bonded from the moment we met in high school. Maybe we were drawn together because what I lacked was what Kristy knew naturally: how to bat her eyes, giggle, and catch any boy she wanted (perfect timing, because I was just realizing I might want to actually date these boys instead of hanging out as their buddy). So Kristy gave me flirting lessons. She had to

w/ Kristy @ my house

be a bridesmaid because I might not have gotten Todd without her. There was no jealousy that I might out-flirt her (not a chance) or steal a boyfriend. She just wanted me to be happy. The bottom line is, Kristy taught me how to flirt.

My other good Lubbock Girlfriend was Rhonda. She is one of the sweetest girls I have ever met. She was actually from a smaller town outside of Lubbock (there's something smaller?). When we met at a speech competition in high school, we knew we'd be lifelong friends. She even got me a date to the Brownfield High School Prom. (Just FYI, I am not a charity case...I just enjoyed meeting people and going to parties. That's my story and I'm sticking to it!) Also, when I came home to Lubbock during the summers while I attended the University of Oklahoma, Rhonda always made sure I was invited to all the big parties and get-togethers. Since I'm an only child and didn't know many of the Texas Tech students, she single-handedly made sure I didn't spend my college summers

w/ Rhonda (left) & our friend Christine (right) in Lubbock during high school

alone and dateless (again, not a charity case!). From Rhonda, I learned there's no substitute for kindness, and real Girlfriends make it look so effortless (and hey, I was able to put Kristy's flirting lessons to good use every summer!).

University of Oklahoma

Ahhh...the college years! I spent five glorious years attending the University of Oklahoma in Norman. (Don't say a word! I had all those years paid for through scholarships, so I took my time). While I was there, I developed several invaluable Girlfriends.

Kappa Alpha Theta pledge class in 1984 @ OU

One I will never forget is my Big Sis, Julie B, in the Kappa Alpha Theta sorority house. (If you aren't familiar with a Big Sis in a sorority, it's basically an upper classman in the house who helps you stay out of trouble, for the most part). Boy, God knew what he was doing when he made Julie my guardian angel! Not only is she straight-laced, but she

23

ended up spending years helping me achieve my dreams. At the time, I was competing for the Miss Oklahoma Pageant, and Julie would go with me to preliminary pageants when my parents couldn't drive all the way from Lubbock. Julie would sometimes help me get ready backstage, but most importantly, she would yell and scream like a mad woman when I got on stage to model a swimsuit or sing for my talent. Julie taught me real Girlfriends are selfless. They never blink an eye to help (no matter how goofy the request), they'll cheer you on like a fool (even if they're the only one clapping for you in the auditorium), and they'll ensure you make good choices. I say that because on the day of my wedding—I freaked out!! Julie and I had a slumber party the night before the big day, and I woke up about five in the morning, hyperventilating. Julie handled me like a pro (which is no easy task!) and gently talked me down from the ledge. She asked me what I liked about Todd and why I thought (before that early morning) I wanted to spend my life with him. What a simple concept! While I wasn't ready for the huge commitment of marrying someone forever (that's a long time!), I really was ready to spend the rest of my life with Todd. Kristy's flirting lessons helped me catch him, and Julie's kindness helped me walk down the aisle to marry him.

w/ Julie B @ OU Theta party

Just like Julie, my Girlfriend Teresa put up with the endless voice lessons, interview coaching, and calls from pageant directors, as well as the usual college stuff like classes and studying. She and I were roommates most of our time at the Theta house. Now, we may have initially ended up as roommates because Teresa was the only one who would put up with me (ha!), but I prefer to think we stayed as roommates most semesters because we enjoyed each other so much. Also, Teresa wasn't like most of the girls in the house. Her mother died when she was young, and her father had a horrible stroke that

w/ Teresa during Rush Week @ OU

left him incoherent most of the time Teresa was in college. She took the weight of her entire family on her shoulders by taking care of all the finances (remember, I don't do numbers, so I was just amazed), eventually burying her father shortly after we graduated from college. I don't know how she did it all. My parents were so supportive and loving that I couldn't imagine my accomplishments without them, and yet Teresa just took things in stride and was a success in spite of her circumstances. Teresa definitely taught me real Girlfriends stand strong in the face of adversity because this too shall pass.

I'm not sure how to explain my Girlfriend and sorority sista, Janna. We were friends in the Theta house but became much closer after graduation. That is when she secured her Bridesmaid status. Janna is tall, blonde, and beautiful (uh, a bombshell!), but yet you'd never know it when you get her into a deep Girlfriend discussion. She's frank and honest, yet not afraid to laugh at herself. Janna is one of my dearest friends (more stories to come about my Glamour

25

w/ Janna our freshman year @ OU

Girls), but her greatest gift before my wedding was honesty. If your Girlfriends don't tell you what looks bad, then who will? (Well, actually my mother would gladly volunteer to tell me, but most of the time she's still in Lubbock and just can't see what I'm wearing.)

Pageants

I already let the cat out of the bag and mentioned I competed in the Miss Oklahoma Pageant (which goes on to Miss America). If you didn't throw the book in the trash then, you probably at least rolled your eyes. (You did, didn't you?) However, as a general manager of a TV station once told me, he would always hire pageant girls because they already knew how to dress, they'd learned to work hard to be the best, and a little competition didn't scare them. See? Modeling that swimsuit in high heels should earn me a little respect, right? All right, moving on...

I guess I should mention that I did not win Miss Oklahoma (although I have crowned myself many times in my own head!). I was actually third runner-up to a good Girlfriend of mine named Cindy. If I couldn't win that year, I was glad she did (no, I really do mean that!). Cindy taught me no matter how hard you work for something, you can be happy and supportive of another Girlfriend if she wins. There was no sabotage between us, just friendship and a definite

26

respect for what the other had accomplished. (I mean, it's only a real Girlfriend who will spray your butt cheeks with that sticky stuff so your swimsuit won't ride up while on stage!) Of course, I was crushed when I didn't win, but I was genuinely happy for her and supported her

*The Finalists in Miss Oklahoma 1990 -
I'm on the far left & Cindy is in the center*

throughout her reign that year. It turned out for the best, honestly. After the pageant, I went back to my brand new job at the ABC affiliate in Oklahoma City as a reporter, and my career took off. Cindy taught me it's okay not to win sometimes, and you should be happy for your Girlfriends when they do.

Pageant Girlfriend Julie K and I became close Girlfriends after she won Miss Oklahoma USA (which goes on to Miss USA). She called and asked for my help preparing for the Miss USA Pageant. (Me? Really?! Well, if you insist!) She and I picked out her clothes, found the best hair and makeup styles, and came up

w/ Julie K preparing for Miss USA

with a workout routine. (She had a body to die for and, believe me, worked for every bit of it!) We laughed, we cried, we bonded. When she had a freak-out moment at Miss USA (who wouldn't when you

27

see forty-nine other girls who look as good as you?), she asked for me to meet her and get her back on target mentally. I was more than happy to drive all night to Wichita to do that. Julie didn't win the Miss USA crown, but she placed in the top swimsuit scores (one of the few petite girls to do so in a sea of six-footers). She also made it to the top finalists, but more importantly, I watched her grow into a confident young woman. From Pageant Julie, I learned there's no greater joy than to share your best trade secrets and advice and watch how it can help your Girlfriend succeed.

Now, my Girlfriend Mignon will leave you in stitches. She is probably one of the Girlfriends I admired most then, and still do now. Like my Girlfriend Janna, Minnie is still in my life to this

Miss Oklahoma Mignon & me @ a pageant

day. We're often the Three Musketeers in Vegas (you guessed it, more stories to come!). But back then, I was really in awe of Mignon. When she was Miss Oklahoma, I watched her entertain crowds of people, and not only have them laugh until they cried, but have them in the palm of her hand by the end of the night. I always believe in learning from the best, and Mignon is the best. She helped develop me into the TV personality and public speaker that I am now. Of course, there's so much more to Minnie than "the entertainer." She's a few years older than I am, and when I competed in Miss Oklahoma, I was lucky enough to live with her for a month in order to prepare for the pageant. (A huge thanks goes out to her husband, Stan, since he shared his home and wife's time with me only six months after they were married.) I saw that Mignon's humor drew people to her, but telling a few jokes alone isn't the answer. Mignon is smart (using her pageant scholarships to get a law degree), and she combines it with her humor to actually seal the deal. It has paid off because she is still entertaining crowds of people years after wearing the crown. From my Girlfriend Mignon, I learned smarts and humor are the greatest combination, whether you're in a room of one or thousands.

Work

My final bridesmaid (yes, we're almost done) was my first real work Girlfriend, Sheila. I was hired right out of OU to work at the ABC affiliate in Oklahoma City. That was about two years before Todd and I married. Sheila was head of our promotions department, and I adored her.

w/ Sheila at KOCO Christmas Party in OKC

She was bubbly, always smiling, and very much a "girlie girl." I was new to TV news, and there were some who felt I hadn't really paid my dues since I hadn't worked at a small town TV station for a few years before coming to OKC. But, hey, the news station offered me the job, and I would have been a fool to turn it down, especially since I was making minimum wage at the time, working the makeup counter at Dillard's part-time. If the bosses believed I could do it, then so did I. So did Sheila. When I made a mistake on the air or someone gave me a hard time, Sheila would smile and give me a pep talk. Somehow, between the two of us, I had the courage to keep walking back into that newsroom. I learned from Sheila that not everyone at work is your friend, so when you find that Girlfriend who will truly prop you up and send you back into the fray, then she's a keeper. Sheila taught me that a true friend in the workplace knows it's not a competition, but that it's about supporting another woman to succeed.

Now you can see why I had nine bridesmaids at my wedding. They each had made such a huge impact on my life. By the age of twenty-five, I was ready to start a new family of my own, and these Girlfriends gave me the perfect wedding gifts to continue on the rest of my life journey:

- How to flirt (which has now developed into making a real connection when I talk one-on-one with someone)

- There's no substitute for kindness (I'm a big believer in Karma—nice girls really do win)

- Be selfless with those who really matter (this one definitely comes in handy as a mother)

- Have strength in the face of adversity (uh, like a layoff)

- Honesty is the best policy (just check out some of my old investigative "gotcha" reports on YouTube—the bad guy always gets caught)

- It's okay not to win sometimes (life is a marathon not a sprint, and sometimes there's a better prize down the line)

- Always share your best trade secrets in the Girlfriend Network (you are guaranteed to feel wonderful)

- Be witty by combining smarts and humor (laughter is truly the best medicine)

- Girlfriends should not be in competition with each other (help others get what they want, and you will get what you want)

All of these bridesmaids helped make me the Girlfriend I am today, and I thank them. They also have another thing in common: they're all "10s." I'm a big believer that if you want to be a "10," you need to surround yourself by "10s." Think about it. If you're a "7" and surround yourself by "5s," "6s," and "7s" because you want to be the smartest in the room, you're doing yourself a disservice. You're never going to be better, richer, or happier, much less grow as a person. No, if you truly want to be a success, surround yourself by "10s." They won't be intimidated to help you. They will pick you up when you stumble and fall, and over time they will make you a better person. Think about it. All great leaders never truly believe they're the be-all-end-all. Instead, they know they're only as good as the people with which they surround themselves. There's little doubt, my bridesmaids were (and still are!) absolute "10s." I'd like to think it's because birds of a feather flock together, but I think that is probably giving myself way too much credit at a young age. No, I think I've always admired and wanted to be with those successful girls who are willing to share, help, and laugh. There's no competition. There's no holding back. We help each other reach our full potential because we love each other. That theme has carried through the rest of my life. Now I knowingly surround myself by only the best Girlfriends possible, and I think my first group of gal pals made that a prerequisite.

All ten of us being silly w/ our white fur muffs @ the 1991 wedding

Here's your very first Girlfriends Challenge:

1. Make a list of what your past and present Girlfriends have taught you. It really does make an impact when you see it on paper.

2. Why not let those Girlfriends know the gifts they've given you that will last a lifetime? I've loved sharing what I've discovered through my journey and this book.

3. Make sure you're surrounding yourself by the best Girlfriends possible ("10s") so you'll be the best you can be. (In other words, if you're the smartest, brightest, and most successful person in the room at all times, there's a problem, Girlfriend.)

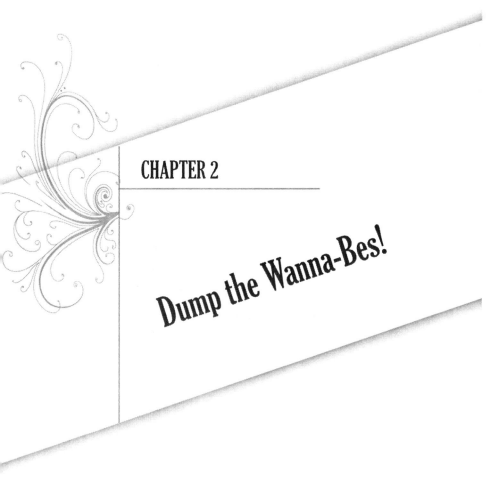

CHAPTER 2

Dump the Wanna-Bes!

I believe becoming a true and trusted Girlfriend is something you learn and earn over time. Let me restate that…you learn and earn Girlfriend status. I don't believe it's something you are born knowing. Remember those mean girls in high school? Yes, some of them may still be mean, but I'll bet at your last reunion, most of them had learned to respect their friends and are better, kinder people because of it. I know as I get wiser (using the word "older" involves Botox), I learn to be a better mom, wife, worker, and Girlfriend, many times because of the influence of my Girlfriends. That's why a good Girlfriend can make all the difference. On the other hand, a bad girlfriend (notice no capitalization) can be a cancer that can, or will at least try to, destroy you. This is the perfect time to tell you that not all girlfriends are created equal. Choose wisely.

Blessed with really great Girlfriends
like Debby, Jennifer and Tracy

Maybe because I've been blessed with really great Girlfriends, I used to be under the false impression that anyone can be one. Wrong! That naive thinking has burned me more than once. This chapter is not about revenge (well, maybe a little); instead, it's about the importance of keeping your good Girlfriends close and dumping those who "wanna be" your friend but either don't know how or don't have your best interests at heart. Oh, I should mention, I'm changing the names to protect the guilty.

Sabotage Suzie

Seriously, in pageants I didn't see half the back-stabbing behind the scenes that I saw from a few co-workers behind closed doors. When it involves a much needed paycheck and someone's career, I guess some people get a little nasty and territorial. (Let me make this perfectly clear—that's not how I roll because my mother taught me better!) However, I will never understand someone who actually befriends you and then turns on you. That's the lowest. I always imagine Suzie Sabotage saying "Oh I'm sorry...did my knife land in your back?" Uh, yeah. It landed right where you were aiming, Little Missie!

In twenty years of television, I have had awesome Girlfriends at work: Sheila (my bridesmaid), Tracy, Kay, and the ever supportive

DC. But I have also met some pretty expert Sabotage Suzies at work who I thought were friends. One almost ended my ever wanting another Girlfriend at work—period. We were not only friends, but our kids had play dates. I remember girls at the station warning me she was out for herself, but I didn't listen. (Note to self: listen next time!) I also noticed she didn't have any other real Girlfriends. (That is one of the biggest red flags!) Regardless, I went out of my way to hold her hand through some really rough times and did nothing but support her. However, in a last ditch effort to keep her job, she had some closed-door meetings with the bosses, claiming I didn't work as hard as she did, that she was a better journalist, and even insinuating that I was having an affair with a co-worker. Oh, no, she didn't! When the bosses told me she'd said that, I couldn't distance myself fast enough from Suzie, but I was honestly devastated. How could she say something like that when we were friends, and she knew it wasn't true? That's when I realized you can't teach or change a Sabotage Suzie. These girls have no friends because they have no clue how to be one themselves. If you get even the slightest hint you might have a Suzie in your life, run (do not walk!) to the nearest exit. She just can't help herself, and she will eventually sabotage you in one way or another.

And here's where I have to admit something. If a so-called friend puts something as precious as your family in the crosshairs, it's hard to truly forgive. Although I'd dumped Suzie physically, I still let her affect me mentally. And that, my dear Girlfriends, was my fault. Unfortunately, I didn't realize that she was still under my skin until years later. I can only hope my "ah ha!" moment will save you the heartache I endured. You see, I unknowingly carried around the hurt and anger about Suzie until recently, when a trusted confidante called my bluff. My Mentor and Friend, David, saw the truth in my humor one day and told me that until I let go of Suzie and whoever else I was ticked off at, I wouldn't be free. Even worse, how could I lead other women to freedom if I was still bound by my own emotional chains? Whoa....

You know what I did? I cried...not just a little, but a lot! I needed to grieve. I needed to get past the anger and bitterness of her betrayal years before and simply mourn the loss of someone I had cared about. That is the day I really dumped Suzie for good. The next day, I felt at peace and empowered. Please don't let a Suzie Sabotage or anyone else hold you emotionally hostage. It will poison you to your core. Instead, dump that person entirely, and then you really can get on with living your own life. But a word of caution: forgive, but do not forget! Your memory will prevent you from making the same mistake again. I will never let Suzie Sabotage back into my Girlfriend network, but I can now run into her and genuinely hug her children and warmly greet her. I wish her only the best professionally and personally (and now I actually mean it). Thank goodness my book didn't go to print before I learned about true forgiveness. Girlfriend, try it. It really will set you free!

Helen Hater

I was blindsided one fall by an expert Helen Hater when my son played football in the fourth grade. I did not volunteer for "Team Mom," but somehow ended up getting "nominated" (remember my problem with saying "no"?). So, I handled that position just like

I would my job—professionally, 100 percent, and over the top. I helped get sponsors to make sure boys who couldn't afford their dues or uniforms were taken care of. I had a parents' party at my house so we could all get to know each other. I spent hours creating and updating a team website. I even made sure every boy would walk away with tons of free stuff: t-shirts, a big party, photos, and a team poster. What did I get for all that effort? Happy players and Helen Hater.

First, she apparently started a rumor that I was embezzling team funds to go on vacay in Hawaii. (Huh? I doubt our team bank account would have gotten me to Dallas and back on Southwest Airlines!) I was in shock! Remember, I'm not a numbers person so I kept very detailed and open records. Besides, me steal from nine-and ten-year-old boys? Oh, puhlease! Last I checked (back then) I had a full-time job—unlike Helen Hater!

Her second strike? Convincing the coach my husband was saying bad things about the coach's son. Well, anyone who knows Todd knows he just wouldn't do something like that. When I tried to talk with Coach about it, he refused to listen. That's when I realized that I may play a professional person on TV, but I was no match for Helen Hater. The hours I'd spent, the stuff I'd paid for, the effort I'd gone to—she didn't care. And, in fact, the more I did, the more venom she spread. I learned right then, you cannot stop a Helen Hater any more than you can stop Sabotage Suzie. So I took the best course of action I could think of; I resigned as team mom. Did she win? Maybe. I certainly got lots of cards and calls from the other (innocent) parents, which made me feel better, but I didn't do the job of "Team Mom" for them. I did it for the boys. Regardless, that volunteer job wasn't worth the stress Helen Hater caused me, my family, and the team. Do not try to take Helen head on. You will not win. By the way, I learned another valuable lesson. Mark my words: I will never be team mom again!

Just Don't Get It Gidget

When it comes to Gidget, bless her heart. She just doesn't get what it takes to be a Girlfriend or how important Girlfriends are to each other. Nor does she care. She's all about herself and gives nothing in return. If you invest much time in Gidget, you're just spinning your wheels.

My Gidget was successful, pretty, and normal, it seemed, but (again) I should have noticed that she didn't really have any other Girlfriends. (Remember...major red flag!) Unfortunately, several years into our friendship, she began to totally self-destruct. I knew she probably never needed a friend more than at that time, so I tried to help her. I lost several other friends over that controversial choice, but I knew she needed someone to help guide her to a better path. That's what Girlfriends do: when the going gets tough, we get tougher. Anyway, I suggested she deal with her problems before leaving her family, job and sanity behind. However, you can't help someone who doesn't want help, no matter how desperate she may be. In the end, she lost her husband, home, and job. I physically got ill over her self-destruction, but you know what? She quickly moved on from her train wreck and quit returning my calls. If someone doesn't "get" what it takes to be a real friend, she won't appreciate your efforts and you are the one who will lose sleep over it.

Needy Nancy

Ugh! This one exhausts me just thinking about her. You may not see a Sabotage Suzie, Helen Hater, or Just Don't Get It Gidget coming...but a Needy Nancy is easy to spot from the get-go. I have dealt with several of these women over the years. You may also know her by a different name: Draining Dorothy. They are HIGH maintenance and will take, take, and take. They also love to play the guilt card...ugh!! My saving grace is that I have not had a Needy Nancy or Draining Dorothy in my life for long. With my hours at work and kids' activities, these so-called friends usually don't last long with me. For instance, I had one Needy Nancy tell me that if a friend missed two of her parties, then she was off the invite list. Needless to say, she's wealthy and never worked a day in her life. I laughed and reminded her (at the time) I worked weekend nights in TV and probably wouldn't be able to attend any parties even though I wanted to. Needless to say, I never got another invite. Her loss....

When it comes to Friends, I always use this analogy: if your cup is full of water and you keep giving everyone a drink (parents, husband, kids, Girlfriends, work), you'll soon end up with an empty cup. Then you can't give anyone a drink, much less yourself. Even the airlines say, "Put the mask on yourself before you put it on your child." There's wisdom in that. You need to always take time to refill your cup. Kids will unknowingly suck it dry, right along with

Needy Nancy. The difference is your kids don't know any better. Real Girlfriends know friendship is a give and take. If my cup starts running on empty, I always know one of my Girlfriends will alert me that I'm running dry, or they'll simply fill it for me without asking or expecting a thank you (it's the same wonderful philosophy my Girlfriends use for wine, too). Those who know only how to "take" don't care if you're running on empty, and, in fact, that's usually when they have the audacity to drain your cup and ask you to get them more. (Thus the name Draining Dorothy...clever, huh?) Don't fall for it. And yes, sometimes even your best friends will be needy and draining. It's just part of being human, but if it's a pattern, you don't need them.

Gayle Guilt

Boy, have I met my fair share of Gayle Guilts! Oy! Let me tell you, growing up in the South, there is plenty of guilt to spread around. Let's see...I'm a working mom. Guilt! After all the stress, I'm too tired for a little something-something with my husband. Guilt! There are never enough hours in the day to keep up with my precious Girlfriends. Guilt! I'm a People Pleaser, so I can't say no, and I generally end up over-scheduling my schedule. Guilt! Believe me, the list goes on and on and on. So why would I surround myself with people who pile on more guilt than I already pile on myself? The answer is—I don't.

My motto: there should be no guilt in true Friendship. When friends deal the guilt card because I'm busy or haven't talked with them in the amount of time they deem important, I'm done! Honestly, I love and adore my Girlfriends, but I also have a job and family that have to come first. As women, we do what we can do, right? So, if you can't understand that, then I'm thinking we're not really Girlfriends. I can't answer every call, and I can't be there every second of the day. The caveat to that, of course, is if you really need me or there's an emergency, then I'll drop everything and be there for you in the blink of an eye! However, since most of us barely have time to have a meaningful conversation with our husbands, sometimes friendships have to go on the backburner for awhile. It doesn't mean our dearest friendships aren't important; it just means that in life's busy juggling act there are only so many balls we can have in the air at one time and stay sane. The bottom line is that we're all busy and life happens. I can't ignore my obligations, and I refuse to let any friend make me feel guilty about that. Period.

Competitive Cathy

Growing up, I played tennis. I had a great poster in my room of Snoopy with a racket saying "Winning isn't everything, it's the only thing." It always made me laugh because (a) who doesn't love Snoopy, and (b) it's funny. Well, at least I thought it was funny. Some women think of it as a life lesson, and heaven forbid you get in the way. Competitive Cathy wants what you have because she believes winning really, really is the only thing (and she's ready to win at all costs). She just can't stand to see someone else in the spotlight (and she's blinded by that), or she's jealous. (Jealous Jessica raises her head from the depths of high school once again!)

43

Unfortunately, I have met many Competitive Cathy types in the news business over the years, but few were ever really considered a Girlfriend. The exception was one co-worker who filled my anchor position while I was on maternity leave. During that time, she had the gall (wait till you hear this!) to call and tell me that management was so pleased with her performance filling in on my 5 p.m. news, they wanted me to extend my leave so *she* could fill in a little longer! Hello?! Could you kick a woman any more when she's down? At that point I had plenty of baby fat to share, I was exhausted and overwhelmed, and I probably hadn't had the time or energy to take anything more advanced than a spit bath. It's just a good thing Competitive Cathy called instead of showing up in person, because she might not have had a hair on her head left! Considering the depth of my sleep deprivation, I thought I handled the phone conversation well. Afterward I bawled my eyes out, then called my New York City agent.

When I calmed down enough to talk in a pitch that more than just dogs could hear, Carol (my agent) set me straight. "Cindy, you may think she's your girlfriend, but until management calls personally to extend your leave, don't buy it." Suddenly I realized my Girlfriend (with a "G") had become my girlfriend (with a "g"). While Competitive Cathy told me months earlier she was gunning behind the scenes for an anchor slot, I never dreamed it would be *mine*! In one fell swoop I knew I could no longer trust her because she had made this a competition. Who won? Well, let's just say that management never called me to extend my time off, and when I returned to work as scheduled, my anchor chair was waiting for me. She eventually alienated herself from all the female anchors and finally left the station.

True friendship is not a competition...ever. (If you doubt that, please refer to the Bridesmaid chapter.) I'm not just talking at work. Men, status, money, success...there's no room for competition if you're truly friends. For instance, I have a Girlfriend named Heidi

w/ Girlfriend Heidi during an evening out & about

who is a model. Yep...perfect body, face, and teeth. I would actually avoid standing next to her altogether if she wasn't so dang nice! No, seriously, Heidi is absolutely beautiful and has signs, posters, and ads all over town. And you know what? I'm neither jealous nor do I feel I have to compete with her for my self-worth. In fact, I take great pride in her accomplishments, and I'm thrilled to share those moments with a woman who has a heart of gold. For her part, Heidi couldn't be more jazzed about my award-winning TV career. It's not successful model vs. prime time news anchor...it's two Girlfriends who are thrilled to see the other reach their true potential.

Being a Girlfriend is about empowering, embracing, and supporting each other. Instead of Snoopy, think more along the lines of Zig Ziglar. In college, my older (and much wiser) Girlfriend Debbie gave me this quote from the legendary motivational speaker: "You will have everything in life you want...if you will help other people get what they want." Please re-read that sentence. It's powerful! There is more than enough room in the Girlfriend Network for everyone to be successful and get what they want. If you're a contributor to someone's success, then you win as well.

It's that simple. So if someone is jealous or somehow makes your friendship a competition, forget it and dump 'em. They are more concerned about beating you than celebrating your success, and that means they'll never, ever genuinely be happy for you. What a waste of your time!

Tit-for-Tat Tammy

Having worked sixty-hour weeks for most of my kids' lives, I realize they have never known anything different than someone else picking them up from school and getting them to (and sometimes from) football, baseball, cheer, and dance. While we have our go-to babysitter, Miss Rover, there's no doubt that I have leaned heavily on my Girlfriend Network to help me with my children over the years. I can't thank these Girlfriends enough: Marquita, Jennifer, Tricia, Gayle, Courtney, Julie, Sue, and Cindy, just to name a few. They have never counted how many times they bailed me out and never made me feel guilty (Gayle Guilt territory). I'm blessed to have these special ladies in my life. Without them, I would have driven myself (and my family) crazy.

But Tit-for-Tat Tammy is notorious for always keeping score of who does what, and wanting an "eye for an eye." These chickie-poos wear me slick! I mean, who really cares how many times your kid spends the night or who last paid for lunch? Life is too short for that kind of silly stuff! If you're truly Girlfriends, you are always there for each other, and it all balances out in the end. While I may not be able to run the carpool for Girl Scouts once a month, I try to be extra helpful on weekends. If I know money is running tight for a Girlfriend, then I'll pick up lunch. No strings, no retribution, no tally sheet.

So what's a big red flag to spot for a Tit-for-Tat Tammy? She's notorious for complaining about small friendship inequities to anyone who will listen. Yep, if someone is always talking about how they are so "put upon" by a friend, chances are they're not a doormat but instead a friend with a score card. If a friendship really has become lopsided or someone feels taken advantage of (which can happen even in the best of Friendships), then quit complaining and sit down for a good heart-to-heart conversation. It's amazing what that can accomplish between two people who really care for each other.

Abigail Agenda

Being in a high profile career, I have met more than my fair share of women who befriended me not because of my stellar personality (ha!), but instead for their own agenda. As far as life in general, Abigail is not overly harmful because, while she is a user, she will eventually move on without causing too much damage. Just don't let her into your trusted and dependable inner Girlfriend circle because she will waste your precious time (by taking up space in your head but never paying rent), and she'll never be there for you when you really need her.

Maybe because I have been so blessed with great, giving Girlfriends in the past, I usually have a hard time spotting Abigail Agenda until her mission is accomplished and she's nowhere to be found. That's where you can have reinforcements. My Girlfriend Sue is my Abigail Agenda watchdog. She's extremely protective of me because of my job and does not appreciate anyone who has a hidden agenda. But believe me you don't have to be on TV to attract this kind of user. Abigail only wants to get close to you because of something you can do for her: raise her status, make her appear to have more money, tell her gossip, get a promotion, or anything else she deems important. She methodically worms her way into your life, takes what she wants when she wants it, and then she scatters to the wind.

When my news director told me in January the station might not be able to afford me anymore, I found I did still have a few Abigail Agendas in the outskirts of my Girlfriends Circle. Only true Girlfriends will stick by you during a real tragedy because, let's face it, there's nothing glamorous about tears, fears, and midnight phone calls. My few Abigails headed for more stable ground until they could see whether I would retain any "celebrity status." Whatever! You need to make sure you only surround yourself with people who love you for you, not because of something you are, do, or have. Agendas come and go, but real Girlfriends are there through thick and thin, fat and skinny, or rich and poor.

Debbie Downer

I forgot about this one until I was having a discussion with my Girlfriend Melanie. I was telling her my take on the Girlfriend Wanna-Bes and why they should be dumped ASAP. She reminded me that Debbie Downers should get tossed to the curb, too. Debbie is one who is always down. Now I'm not talking depressed or blue, because I went through that after having each of my kids. My (very wise) Girlfriends were the ones who convinced me I needed to see a doctor so I could get better. Actual depression is far different than Debbie Downer. She's one who's never happy, never satisfied, and whines all the dang time. Seriously, you could give Debbie the world and she'd complain about the work it takes being Queen. I have little time for that. Debbie needs to put on her big-girl panties and deal with it!

If I've learned anything these last five months, it's that the attitude of your Girlfriends can help you set your sails or leave you in a boat without an oar. You need Girlfriends who are positive about themselves, you, and life. They can help build you up when you're down. They'll also tell you to shut up when you're whining too much (although a little whining every once in awhile is a Girlfriend's right). Unfortunately, Debbie Downer will always bring you down to her level. You know what I say about that? Buh-bye....

Since I outlined the fab qualities of my Bridesmaids at the end of the last chapter, I better outline the "yikes" qualities of Wanna-Bes:

- Suzie Sabotage can't help but stab you personally or professionally (it's simply in her DNA).

- Helen Hater will never like you (don't take her on because you will not win).

- Just Don't Get It Gidget will never get what friendship means (*you* will lose sleep, not her).

- Needy Nancy will drain the life right out of you (and will most likely guilt you to death at the same time).

- Gayle Guilt doesn't understand there is never guilt in a friendship...ever. (Seriously, we're lucky to be sane since we're all just holding it together with duct tape and twine some days.)

- Competitive Cathy never celebrates you but instead always tries to "one up" you (apparently she never got the Girlfriend Handbook, huh?).

- Tit-for-Tat Tammy is always keeping score of who did what and will constantly complain about what you haven't done (obviously she has nothing better to do).

- Abigail Agenda is out for herself and will leave you high and dry once she uses and abuses you to get what she wants (heaven forbid she break even so much as a nail helping you).

- Debbie Downer is, well...a downer (and she certainly prefers company at that level).

Are there more names than these? Absolutely! Off the top of my head these names come to mind:

- Nanette Know-It-All

- Deedee Drama

- Told-You-So Tina

- Wear Out Wanda
- Gloria Gossip
- Lying Linda

You know exactly who I'm talking about, sista! No matter what their names, you need to dump them, and dump them fast. Now, that does not mean you have to be rude or verbally analyze their "issues" as you back peddle out of the relationship. That's just petty, silly and something Told-You-So Tina would do. Instead, just gracefully "quit" the friendship. It's okay to simply dump someone who threatens to suck you dry. Remember, these women are emotional vampires who don't want you to succeed, whether consciously or subconsciously. And once you have physically and mentally said "buh-bye," please make sure you don't invite in another Wanna-Be to take her place. I can guarantee you, while I have experienced each and every one of these so-called "girlfriends" in the past, not a one of them is in my life today.

At this stage of my life and in this economy, I definitely need Girlfriends (2.0) who make me a better person. So you see, we really do get wiser with age. In my 20s, I thought I needed to have a lot of friends to be valuable. In my 30s, I thought I had to stick by my friends no matter what antics they played. In my 40s, if I get even the hint that you don't have other really good Girlfriends, that you might stab me or that you're a hater—forget it! I don't have the time or energy for you in my 2.0 Girlfriend network! It's a new day, Girlfriend! Quality (not quantity) counts. So unite and dump the Wanna-Bes!

Your second Girlfriends Challenge:

1. Who have been your emotional vampires in the past? Dump them completely (physically and mentally) and get on with it. We all live and learn....

2. Who threatens to suck the life out of you now? Cut your losses while you still can.

3. I challenge you, from now on, to spot these people who "wanna be" your friend but can't for whatever reason, and avoid them before you get sucked in. Only surround yourself by friends who filleth your cup.

CHAPTER 3

Don't wear that!

Okay, we've wasted enough time talking about those who want to be your friends but don't have what it takes to make it over the long haul. So let's get back to the good Girlfriend stuff. Let me tell you, my first real Girlfriend is my mother, Betty Wall. We always had a blast shopping together when I was growing up. Sometimes we'd even go out of town and shop for days, looking for just the right school clothes, pageant gown, or jeans. (See? Girlfriend shopping excursions and vacays are in my genes!) Well, those early experiences made me realize, and appreciate the fact, that only a girl who truly cares about you will really tell you what looks good on you and what doesn't. My precious mother now lives a state away (whimper!) so I now get my best fashion ideas and no-no's on a daily basis from my Girlfriends. In fact, I think it is no mere coincidence that one of my

Mom, Marlowe & Me on vacation

Girlfriends (Mignon) gave me my first subscription to the "Fashion Bible"—*InStyle* Magazine. That ranks right up there with my mother buying my first subscriptions to the fashion magazines *Teen* and *Seventeen* while I was growing up!

These days, though, there is a definite advantage to hearing "Puhlease don't wear that!" from your Girlfriends. Their advice usually doesn't come with baggage, strings, or a history. Let's face it, now that I'm in my 40s, sometimes it stings when my mother mentions something doesn't look good. That kind of comment is usually followed by a fifteen minute diet conversation (which I do not want to have in front of a three-way mirror, thank you very much) or a talk about how forty-year-olds should not try to dress like they are in their 20s. (This is where I tend to ruin a perfectly good shopping trip by reminding my mother that I'm mature enough to run a household, care for a family, and tell half a state what's going on in the world around them. They trust me...why doesn't she? Uh, yeah...baggage? It's the child saying "I am Woman, hear me roar!" Sorry, Mom). That is mild, though, compared to my husband being innocent (read: stupid!) enough to tell me something doesn't look right. Need I remind Todd of the day we were leaving the hospital with our newborn son, and he decided to casually ask why I was still wearing my maternity sweats instead of the jeans I wore pre-pregnancy. D'oh!! Girls, I couldn't make this stuff up! And then there was the time, three months later, when supermodel Cindy Crawford bragged on one of the morning shows about how she'd lost her baby fat in that amount of time. My husband, toothbrush in mouth, innocently turned to me and said, "See, most moms can do it in three months." Poor thing...he had no idea the wrath he was bringing upon himself. No wonder it was almost three years later before we had our daughter (ha!), and actually, he's lucky at the time that toothbrush didn't become a permanent part of his brain. (No female jury would have ever convicted me!) Needless to say, I never

know what he thinks these days because he keeps his mouth shut, so apparently I trained him well. (Good boy!) Anyway, when Girlfriends say something doesn't look right, it is simply fact. There isn't any sarcasm, guilt, or ulterior motives. It just is what it is. It doesn't look good. Okay... then I'll change clothes.

w/ Mignon (left) & Janna (middle) in Vegas

On one of my recent trips to Vegas with my Bridesmaids Mignon (who lives in Kansas) and Janna (who lives in Oklahoma City), we were trying to find an outfit for me to wear to emcee a huge gala back in Tulsa. We searched, but I was a few pounds over what I wanted to be (aren't we always?), and we couldn't find anything we liked. Oh actually, I'm going to get side-tracked for a moment (shocker!). If you have anything big — a date, anniversary, gala, job interview — take your best Girlfriend fashionistas with you. First of all, you're guaranteed at least one glass of wine during the afternoon. Secondly, you're bound to break into giggles in at least one fitting room. And most importantly, your Girlfriends will help you pick something that looks good from all sides. They're not there on commission (never blindly trust a salesperson), and they don't look at things through flattering lights and skinny mirrors (although I think they should be required in every store). Instead, your Girlfriends leave little to chance when picking out the right outfit for something important. They will have you turn around, sit down and walk, just to make sure it's perfect. They'll also make sure you have the proper stylish undergarments to look sucked, tucked, and put together. The only other person I know who does that just because she loves me is my mom. But again, she's in Lubbock, Texas, and I'm in Tulsa,

Janna and Me

Oklahoma, so it's a little hard to take her shopping on a whim, so I always head out to shop with the Girls. If they can't go with me, then I'll try on the outfit for them at the house. Their house or mine, it doesn't matter. If they don't likee—it goes backee.

All right, back to Vegas and the gals I refer to as my Glamour Girlfriends. Since the stores were a bust, we hit Janna's suitcase. Now mind you, we're on vacay, but Janna always seems to get the most incredible clothes into the smallest suitcase possible. Also, Janna is one of those wonderful Girlfriends who loves to share. In fact, a few years ago in Vegas, Janna had this top I just loved and I wore it several times. Since then, my thoughtful Girlfriend brings it for me to wear every year. However, we decided that top wasn't right for the big Tulsa gala, so we dug deeper into her amazing and magical suitcase. Sure enough, she pulled out two rocking evening gowns. They were hip, elegant, and to die for. Of course, what I've neglected to make clear again since the Bridesmaid Chapter is Janna is 5'9—I am not. While I might be able to pull off one of her fab tops, an evening gown is a different story. That became apparent when, after stripping off my clothes and trying on the first one, Janna nixed it right away with something close to "Oh, hell no!" We decided the second one might be right with really high heels and some major power Spanx beneath it, so maybe we could call off the search for the perfect dress. (By the way, if you are wondering what Spanx are you either: (1) don't need them, or (2) need a little Girlfriend insight and must check them out on the Internet right away!) Anyhoo, during this whole fiasco, our third Girlfriend was strangely quiet. (Hmmmm...that's suspicious because Mignon is never quiet.) Later, at lunch, Janna leaned over and said, "Mignon doesn't want to hurt your feelings, so she didn't say anything. But she told me that I can't let you borrow that dress because it doesn't look good." God, I love my Girlfriends. Whether you're a Janna-type and not shy to call it as you see it, or a Mignon-type who doesn't blurt it out but still makes sure you get the message, my peeps made sure I didn't wear something that didn't make me look my absolute best. So, what did I end up wearing to the big gala? I recycled an old standby in my closet that was already Girlfriend approved.

I also have two tried-and-true Girlfriends here in Tulsa who do outfit checks. First, I can always call on my Girlfriend Aunt Sue (she got the name "Aunt Sue" after my kids were born, because

"Aunt Sue" & me @ church

she is their godmother). She's a "less-is-more" kind of gal, while I'm a "more-the-merrier" kind of dresser. She wears more black, and I like to be bold with color, so we're the perfect ones to help each other get ready for a big event. Sue had a wedding a few years back and was going to see family and friends she hadn't seen in forever (time to impress without looking like you tried). Sue ripped through her closet trying on clothes while I sat on the bed playing judge and jury (how the outfit looks when you walk away is extremely important, by the way). Finally we decided on a darling little black dress with heels and pearls (classic!), but it was almost too much of an "over-forty-years-old" uniform. That's where I earned my keep as a Girlfriend. I rushed home and got her a hot pink cashmere wrap to pack. Sure enough, the wedding was a bit chilly and Sue looked smashing with her pop of pink. On the other hand, she is my fashion voice of reason. She's the first to remove at least one necklace I've put on or remind me that you can wear too many statement pieces. (Really?)

My other clothes horse is my Girlfriend Cindy H. (This is not the Bridesmaid Cindy. This Cindy is one of my dearest friends who earned that distinction after we were introduced by our inseparable sons.) She and I can shop till we drop! Our shopping excursions usually include a glass of wine, but not too much or everything we try on looks good (ha!). We also do the same thing when we shop in each other's closets. What more can you ask for? A glass of vino, Girlfriend talk, and previewing outfits! I tell her what looks good and she does the same for me. We also discuss undergarment requirements and jewelry coordination, as well as talk

Cindy H & me @ a basketball game

each other into tossing out what doesn't look good. And let me tell you, I have to have a partner in crime for that. Closet purging is so hard for me! I always rationalize that something might come back into style...or I might wear a size 4 again! You never know....

All of this talk about shopping and clothes goes for hair, makeup, purses, and just about anything else. Don't like your new cut? Before you chew out the hairdresser you've had for decades, run by your Girlfriend's house. Pull out the hair dryer, flat iron, curling iron or whatever, and make sure damage has really been done first. Your Girlfriend can help calm you down emotionally and help you figure out whether it's a cut worthy of a hairstylist breakup, or if your mood swings got the best of you. If the lady at Sephora (my fave!) convinces you to buy $300 worth of new makeup, show it to your makeup maven Girlfriend. She'll tell you if you should really wear glitter after forty or black nail polish in Oklahoma.

Hopefully this chapter will prove that it is your Girlfriends who have the knowledge, insight, and your interests at heart to help you look your best. Honestly, why put your husband or boyfriend in an awkward position by asking him, "Does this look good?" Sometimes he'll unknowingly put his foot in his mouth and then look like a deer in the headlights when you react somewhat like Linda Blair in the movie *The Exorcist*. While a few "dry spells" will teach him faster than Pavlov's dogs that everything looks good on you, it defeats the purpose of knowing whether something really does look good. As for your mother? Only you can decide if your bond is strong enough to survive a session of "Don't wear that!" For me? I love exchanging advice and going on shopping trips with my mother, and why not? She is truly my original homie and one of the most incredible women I know! (Mom, I'll try to check my baggage the next time you give me a suggestion, okay?) I'm already starting down that road with my precious young daughter, Marlowe. As she grows up, I look forward to shopping marathons, shared giggles at an inside joke and teaching her the Girlfriend Code of Conduct. (Oh, I feel another book coming!) No matter your family situation though, you *can* build a Girlfriend base you can (and should) trust in to find out what looks good and what doesn't from top to bottom. Your Girlfriends have nothing to gain but your undying thanks.

So, here's your third Girlfriends Challenge:

1. If you have a good relationship with your mother, I suggest you dust that off and hook up again with your original Girlfriend (she won't always be here!).

2. Figure out which of your Girlfriends are your "go-to girls" for advice and honesty when it comes to what really looks good.

3. If you don't have someone like this in your life, I challenge you to find that person. Remember, it's a give and take relationship so that advice goes both ways.

CHAPTER 4

Girlfriend vacays are a must!

I used to think "girl trips" were a waste of time and money. Why dish out cash to go hang out somewhere with your friends when you don't have enough time with your own family as it is? Well, at least that *was* my thinking before my first few Girlfriend getaways. The first official Girlfriends vacay was a sorority class reunion. We were several years out of school and decided to reunite. I had the time of my life! The Oklahoma City bombing had occurred not too long before that, so I was really stressed (and probably a bit depressed) at work since I had done hours and hours of coverage during the tragedy at my OKC TV station, but all that melted away as we spent the weekend talking about funny college stories, babies, and relationships. I was hooked. (God bless my sweet Thetas!)

The Vegas Glamour Girls (LOL)

By the time my Glamour Girlfriends (and Bridesmaids) Mignon and Janna decided we should all go on a gal's getaway, I couldn't save up the money to buy my plane ticket fast enough. Oh what fun we had! We got to shop/spa/play to our heart's content! In fact, one afternoon we just sat on the floor of our hotel room and played in makeup and traded tips. That is no small thing because our combined makeup and fashion knowledge is second to none! And remember, sharing the inside track on that kind of thing is part of the Girlfriend Code (if you already forgot, you need to reread Chapter One). When I returned home from the time with my Glamour Girlfriends, I felt a bit prettier, sassier, and even more on top of my game, but the effects of this trip were more than skin deep. I felt a new sense of self and (dare I say?) prettier on the inside. We have continued the tradition for years now (maybe eight?), and it is one of the best things I've done for myself.

Something that's interesting to note about my Glamour Girls is that none of us live in the same city anymore. Since we are all busy moms, we don't have much of a chance for the three of us to get together. Vegas is our whole year wrapped into one awesome package. I love it! When Janna, Mignon, and I get together, it's like no time has passed. We pick up where we left off and continue on from there. There's no guilt or shame that the three of us haven't physically had time to get together. Girlfriends shouldn't be high maintenance! Now that doesn't mean we ignore each other the rest of the time. We keep up with each other through text messages, Facebook, and an occasional phone call. But life is busy, so we do what we can. However, if Janna or Mignon needed me in a crisis, I'd be right there in a heartbeat.

Janna was in Tulsa the other day, and we were laughing about some of our Vegas vacay adventures and what I could and could not divulge in the book. (Remember, what happens in Vegas, stays in Vegas!) She did insist I tell one story in particular because it truly shows the depth of our Girlfriend relationship. One day we were in the hotel room, and Janna had her new cell phone in her back pocket (of her very cute jeans, I might add). She kept it there after she'd accidentally left her phone in the public restroom of the Venetian hotel because her fashionable purse was too small to hold lip gloss *and* a phone. Anyway, because we'd spent a good two hours tracking down that dang phone, Janna decided there was no safer spot than the back pocket of her jeans, right? Well, when she pulled her pants down to go to the bathroom…kurplunk! I ran into the bathroom ready to take on a would-be robber when I heard Janna screaming as if she was being attacked. Instead, Janna slid her phone across the bathroom floor and asked me to begin drying it out before it was ruined. Like any good Girlfriend, I scooped up the phone and began Project Dry Phone. I had towels, the dryer, and anything else that might help her brand new phone survive the mishap. It wasn't until Janna was done with her "duty" and washing her hands that it crossed my mind to ask one simple question. "Did the phone fall into the toilet before or after you peed?" Janna broke into hysterics before finally letting me know it fell in before she took care of business. (Whew!) Regardless, it is a true Girlfriend who will grab your wet phone to save it without a thought about where it might or might not have been.

Now let's talk about the Girlfriend trip that changed my life. We have a group of four moms whose kids get along (a bonus), but, more importantly, the moms are best buddies (a must!). We (the moms) really enjoy traveling play dates because it's a great get away for the kids and us. We've done everything together from hanging at the lake to visiting amusement parks. (Dare I mention the weekend in Branson with only one hotel room between all of us?) Well, one summer we decided to rent a villa in Mexico and get away for an entire week. All the other moms were divorced, so I was the only one who had to get a hubby to sign off on the crazy idea. (Four moms and eight kids in a foreign country? What were we thinking?) Despite any obstacles (specifically, my husband), we packed our bags and headed off for some village we couldn't even pronounce. It was funny how the crowds parted at the Puerto Vallarta airport when four moms and eight little kids made our American presence known upon landing. Oh, and I'm pretty sure that sweet little village had no idea what hit it and they won't forget us anytime soon.

Oh my gosh, I forgot to introduce our cast of characters on this trip:

- My Girlfriend Cindy (one of my fashionistas in Chapter Three) and her two sons

- My Girlfriend Carol and her two daughters (one is old enough to babysit, so we weren't totally crazy!)

- My Girlfriend Teresa and her son and daughter

- And then my two kids, Peyton and Marlowe, and me, of course

Okay, on with the story...

When we arrived, the villa was perfect and right on the beach. It was a trip made in heaven. We surfed, boated, and swam day in and day out. My Girlfriend Carol (better known as "Carl"

Kids @ the beach

because of her take-charge attitude) even took all the boys running every morning to keep them conditioned for the upcoming football season. (This is where I say it certainly takes a village to raise kids, because my behind was still in bed while they were exercising at some ungodly hour!). However, the best part was that we had our own built-in babysitter (Carol's daughter) when we weren't "eyes on" with the kids. That meant there was time in the afternoon for us to float in the pool for strictly Girlfriend time. That, for me, was a lifesaver.

Why a lifesaving trip? Glad you asked. You see, at the time, I was having an identity crisis at work. The ABC affiliate in Tulsa originally hired me from Oklahoma City in 1997 to do the five o'clock evening news and head up the investigative unit. I thought (way back then) that the ultimate job was the ten o'clock evening news, which is the most viewed newscast (in our central time zone). That meant nights away from my family, but I rationalized that would be okay because it was "for my career." So when the bosses offered for me to begin the transition into the ten o'clock evening news slot, I was thrilled. At the time, our ten o'clock evening news anchor was ready for a change, and I was ready for the promotion. However, management decided to make a gradual transition since our ten o'clock anchor was an icon and extremely well-respected for her work during the last twenty-five plus years at the station. (Believe me, that is an accomplishment, since TV work could be measured in dog years since our anchor positions rarely last as long as other jobs.) So, the s-l-o-w transition began. I started anchoring the ten o'clock newscast two nights a week, in addition to doing my regular five o'clock evening newscast and investigative stories five days a week. The idea was to stretch out the anchor change over a couple of years. Well, it didn't take me long to figure out that I was doing more work with two less days to do it. Plus, I was missing a lot of my kids' stuff on the two nights I worked late. Wow...anchoring the ten o'clock newscast was not as wonderful as I had dreamed all these years (d'oh!). After a year, I finally went to management and said, "I'm either your ten o'clock girl or not, but either way, I need to concentrate on something all the way instead of trying to do so many things halfway." We finally decided that, for the time being, I would go back to anchoring only the five o'clock evening newscast and do more investigations, and our normal ten o'clock anchor would return to her usual duties. That left me with a bit of an identity crisis. If the ten o'clock newscast had been my ultimate goal for twenty years, and it wasn't now...then what was my brass ring? What was I striving for? And had I failed? All right, so back to Mexico....

While sipping margaritas one afternoon in the pool, I finally broke down and asked my Girlfriends if I was a failure and what was I working toward now? Gosh, I love those Girls! They dished out the advice like candy, and it was everything I needed to hear. My Girlfriend Cindy convinced me that I shouldn't define myself as a success or a failure based on a newscast. Instead, I needed to learn who I was and what I wanted out of life. My Girlfriend Carol insisted I start my own business so I

Teresa (left), Carol (middle) & Cindy H.(right)

wasn't dependent on the station for my work-related happiness and income. (In other words, divide my eggs between a few baskets... just in case.) My Girlfriend Teresa reminded me of all the areas where I am successful—as a mother, wife, journalist, and speaker. They were spot on—I am not defined by my TV job. I'm not defined by the newscast that I anchor. I'm defined by me— who I am as a mother, who I am as a wife, who I am as a journalist. That is who Cindy is! Hear me roar! I am so much more than what viewers might see on TV...and how sad that I wasn't sure of that answer before my Mexico trip.

Now, before you call me a total egomaniac, so caught up in my job that it had become my identity...save your judgments. What is the first question most of us are asked when we meet someone new? "What do you do?" Your answer is followed by either a warm smile from the person asking or a nervous glance at her watch. The fact is our world often defines us by our work (or our husband's work). Are you the rock star at your company? Do you do something intriguing or different? Are you a leader or a follower? Do you volunteer for a cause that's saving the world? Did you leave a high-powered job to raise kids? Is your husband a big wig? People like to put us in a little box and, for twenty years, my unique box was cool...and comfortable. I think it's easy for any of us to "buy into" that, but it was on my Mexico trip that I began to realize it's a slippery slope to believe your own press.

There's little doubt that trip saved my sanity and set the stage for my current journey toward a public layoff. The Reinvention of Cindy began that week in Mexico. I didn't come right back to Tulsa and start a business, but the seeds were planted that week. I came back with a new confidence and a better knowledge of who I was and who I was not. Only my Girlfriends, a week in Mexico, and endless margaritas could have gotten me to that place in my life. I started to see other goals, other opportunities, and a new Cindy on the horizon. Without that Girlfriend's vacay, I'm really not sure how I would have faced my work woes just a couple of years later.

Remember, Girlfriend vacays don't have to last a week, be somewhere exotic, or be something expensive. They can be a weekend at the lake or somewhere convenient where you can solve problems, build bridges, and create bonds that are invaluable. To me, it's like church camp when I was growing up. Sure, the minister's sermons on Sundays were an excellent geiger counter for your life, and youth events were all about learning through fun, but you always came back so inspired to spread the gospel and live a better life after a weekend revival with like-minded kids.

These days, just make sure you don't lose that momentum when your Girls' getaway is over. If you don't live in the same area, make sure you stay in touch through all the wonderful communication tools available today. Think about it—we have cell phones, texting, Facebook and Twitter. There are a 1,001 ways to keep in contact, especially if you live in different places or life gets too crazy. If you live close together, have follow-up dinners to your trip so you stay encouraged, revived, and baptized in the good Girlfriend vibes.

Here's your fourth Girfriends Challenge:

1. Make sure you connect and seek advice from your feel-good Girlfriends who "get it" and can help you make sense of some of life's daunting challenges.

2. Try to plan a Girlfriends vacay or weekend get-together with those most valuable Girlfriends at least once a year or every other year to recharge your batteries. (It doesn't have to be expensive...a simple and old fashioned slumber party might be all you need).

3. Since getting away with *all* your valuable Girlfriends would be impossible, I challenge you, at a minimum, to put your Girlfriends on your "To Do" list and utilize

social media to at least touch base when you're busy. (And even if time passes between chats, there's no guilt because your real Girlfriends know you're there for each other in the blink of an eye, if needed.)

CHAPTER 5

Why guys just don't get it.

Why do we have such incredible friends and most guys don't? Not that guys don't have good friends, but they don't have those soul-baring moments that make our Girlfriends invaluable. Let's face it, girls are not afraid to cry on each other's shoulders, give advice straight from the heart, and help each other succeed. For guys? They have the ultimate 1.0 friendship. Heck, they just need beer, a good sporting event, and conversations limited to commercial breaks. That, to them, is bonding. Whatever! I believe you need actual communication to bond. Grunting, belching, and mug-clinking do not count.

If you don't believe that there's a difference in these same-sex friendships, just ask my dad. (He's a psychologist, so he's

w/ my Dad @ a football game

actually authorized to give expert opinion). Dr. Richard Wall (yep, that's my daddy!) says guys really never have a good friendship role model. Our culture and the media make so many things taboo for men. In fact, he's seen only one relationship on TV that involved two guys truly having real, open and complete bonding like girls do. It's the relationship between Denny Crane (actor William Shatner) and Alan Shore (actor James Spader) on the ABC TV show *Boston Legal.* If you missed the show during its five-year run, you really should rent a season and watch how Denny and Alan engage with each other like true Girlfriends. If one of them was scared then they would have a sleep over. They weren't afraid to talk about their affection for each other, and at the end of the day, they always had a brandy and (gasp!) actually talked! Oh my goodness—either the creator David E. Kelly totally "gets" real friendship or he thought it would make good TV for two guys to be true companions. My dad believes every guy should watch how those two characters sympathize and empathize with each other. Instead, our men insist on having buddies instead of true friends because heaven forbid they show any type of weakness in front of another guy! That is why their male bonding is something fun and fairly frivolous while ours is deep felt and life-changing.

My husband certainly never understood why spending time with my Girlfriends was so important and why every once in a while

I need a "Girl Fix." All that changed when he was invited to be a fly on the wall at one of my book club meetings one weekend. Like many book clubs, ours was really just an excuse to get together and bond. Each month, one Girlfriend would pick a book (whatever!) and host the party to supposedly discuss what we'd learned. (We were supposed to learn? The two books I did read were *Angry Housewives Eating Bon Bons* and *Bitter Is the New Black*.) Anyway, during my month to host the party, I packed all the gals up, and we headed to the lake for a book club meeting in our boat.

This is probably where I should explain something. One thing I do not do is drive the boat...ever! If anything happens to my husband Todd on the lake and it's up to me to save the family, we are in trouble! I'll just have to put down the anchor and pray

My man, Todd, driving the boat

my cell phone works (or hope someone notices me screaming and waving her arms like a mad woman). I'm not going to drive and subsequently sink his boat (which is just my luck!) because that will most definitely bring our marriage to a screaming halt. Because of my "refusing to sink the boat" rule, our girls-only book club had no choice but to ask my husband to join us. However, I sternly warned Todd that during our outing he was under strict orders to only drive the boat and serve drinks. Period! Although I'm quite sure Todd rolled his eyes at my demands, he finally agreed. Hey, why not hang with fifteen bathing beauties and get the inside scoop of what really happens on a Girlfriend getaway? It's rare that testosterone is ever that close to giggles, snorts, and female bonding.

That morning, my sweet hubby loaded up the boat with necessary supplies (alcohol and snacks) and drove us to our favorite cove on Grand Lake. For the most part, Todd pretended to ignore us unless we had a drink request. As the hours wore on, though, it was obvious Todd was intrigued by what he witnessed. We had convinced one Girlfriend to dump her good-for-nothing boyfriend, we'd shared solutions for potty training issues, and we had decided our Girlfriend Teresa wasn't allowed again because she looked too dang good in her bikini (Ha!). We did all that, and it wasn't even noon yet! Then we spent the rest of the day giggling, blowing off steam, and doing more problem solving, and Todd was along for the whole ride. That's when Todd "got it."

He didn't say anything right away. No, he let the lessons he learned that day sink in. A few days later, he told me how impressed he was with the day on the lake. He said we operated as efficiently as any board meeting, and although we passed out advice like a Pez Dispenser, it was always from the heart and usually right on target. (He was glad my Girlfriend dumped her good-for-nothing boyfriend and believed it might not have happened if not for a little Girlfriend intervention on the lake.) Now, of course, Todd is not one to ever relinquish his "man card" even for one second, so when his friends ask for the secret squirrel password for what really happened, he always gives a knowing laugh and says it was boring. But I know better. Great things happen when good Girlfriends get together.

And now when I mention I'm getting together for dinner with my peeps or need a Girlfriend fix, Todd never questions it. He always gives me a kiss and wishes me luck with solving all the world's problems...or at least the problems of the night.

Todd & me @ Grand Lake

Your fifth Girlfriends Challenge:

Hmmmm...this one is difficult. You can't change a leopard's spots. I say this book is about you, so just move on to the next chapter, Girlfriend!

CHAPTER 6

Guyfriends are the new Girlfriends...

After preaching about the fact that men just don't "get" our girlfriend relationships, I guess I should say *most* guys don't get it. There are some guys out there who make great Girlfriends. I know that sounds strange, but just like forty is the new thirty and pink is the new black, the right Guyfriend can be the new Girlfriend. In fact, if you're only picking your Girlfriends based on gender alone, you're missing out on a wealth of knowledge, not to mention a different perspective. Be warned, though. It is a rare and special breed of male who can love you in spite of the fact that you're a girl and there are no fringe benefits...almost a brotherly relationship. Think this can't happen? Read on, sista!

I've always had best Guyfriends, dating back to elementary school. Okay, part of that was because I was a total and complete tomboy until junior high (much to my mother's despair). But even after I discovered boys were cute, I still had my best guy buds. In fact, I was one of the select girls in high school who was actually invited to hang out on boys' poker nights. Maybe those wonderful trustworthy boys made more of an impression than they knew. (God bless them!) With such wonderful Guyfriend experiences early on (notice…capital "G"), I've never really had a second thought about having select guys in my inner circle.

Bradley (left) w/ his date & Todd (in the hat) during the early 90s

Todd got indoctrinated into the whole Guyfriends idea when we met. When I figured out Todd was a keeper, I introduced him to my Girlfriends, as well as to my Guyfriend, Bradley. Although Bradley and I hadn't been close friends in our Texas high school, we quickly became each other's lifeline during college at OU. If I ever needed a guy's perspective while away at school, I always called Bradley. That close friendship continued after college. Although, I have to tell you, Todd and I had a huge hiccup over the whole Guyfriends thing about three months into our relationship. We rented the movie "When Harry Met Sally." Oh dear! Just about the time I had convinced my darling Todd that Bradley and I were just friends, there's a hit movie about two best friends who eventually fall in love (you've got to be kidding me!). Though a fab movie, it set me back six months! With time and trust, Todd began to realize that besides him (of course), I'd always have another "guy" in my life.

In fact, I recently ran into Bradley at our twenty-fifth high school reunion. Over the last eighteen years, he had moved to a different state, and frankly we had just lost touch. When I saw him from across the room, I couldn't wait to give him a big hug. Literally, it was like no time had passed. I was full of pride talking with him. As he filled me in on those missing years, his achievements were no surprise to me. He's not only an incredibly successful businessman, but he's a best-selling author and has a beautiful family. It's funny how so many things came full circle as we talked that night and the next day. We keep in touch now. I really have always surrounded myself with "10s." There's no guilt if time passes before our paths cross again, because we truly do pick up right where we left off as if time stood still in between. Guyfriends definitely are the new Girlfriend. Wow, I love it when I realize I've been stumbling through life and somehow have managed, with the grace of God, to get it right sometimes.

If you think Bradley is my only Girlfriend who happens to be a guy, you are mistaken. Out of the almost ten years I spent at the ABC affiliate in Oklahoma City, I came away with two lifelong friends. One is my Girlfriend Tracy, who also was an anchor and lived right around the corner from me. Tracy and I could talk about anything and always supported one another. My other best Girlfriend? Mick. Mick and I anchored the morning and noon newscasts together for years.

Mick & his wife Lisa (left) @ my OKC going-away party

During that time, why wouldn't we have become dear friends? He's one of the smartest, most caring people I know. And boy, did he care for me during those years we worked together. I'm *so* not a morning person, which makes it rather hilarious that I even did a morning newscast. Our show started at 6 a.m., but I'm pretty sure I wasn't fully awake until about 10 a.m. Mick is always in a good mood, no matter the time, and always made the mornings as pleasant as possible for me. Mick is also the best "people person" I've ever met. Seriously, if I had any kind of issue with a co-worker, friend, or life in general, I could always help solve it with Mick's advice. Plus, we were just about the only two people up at 3 a.m. and done with work by 2 p.m., so we'd hang out and hit golf balls behind the station or go see a movie together in the afternoon. I valued that Girlfriend time because it honestly was like hanging with any of my girl homies. He had my back, he wanted nothing but the best for me, and I always felt safe and secure with him.

When I left Oklahoma City for a main anchor job in Tulsa, my friendship with, and advice from, Mick never stopped. For years I've gotten goofy and hilarious gifts from him in the mail (how he ever found a Jessica the Journalist Barbie, I'll never know!). He sends me an encouraging or funny text almost weekly, which always leads to great texting banter or a phone call. Mick is amazing and (although he blushes when I say it) he's pretty much a hero to me. He left TV and started a political career. He quickly went from City Councilman to the mayor of Oklahoma City! Best of all, he has won re-election by the greatest margin of any mayor in the city's history. (Can you tell how proud I am of him? I told you he was an excellent people-person and problem-solver!) I've been gone from Oklahoma City for a dozen years now, but Mick certainly is a valuable part of my Girlfriend network that I wouldn't have if I had only picked on gender alone.

If you think these guys are embarrassed or humiliated by the Girlfriend title, think again. After I moved to Tulsa, my Oklahoma City Girlfriends threw me a shower for my first pregnancy. Guess who was first on the invite list? You guessed it—Mick. That's right... thirty women and him. Most guys would be embarrassed and flat out ignore the invitation, but not Mick. He was there hanging out with all my other good Girlfriends, and he never batted an eye. He laughed with us, "ooohed" and "ahhhed" at the gifts, and did the whole girl thing (although I'm pretty sure his wife picked out the gift). But the point is he knew I wanted and needed him to come to the shower. He was part of my inner circle, so how could I have such a huge celebration without him? But to face that all-female crowd? I truly appreciate his sense of humor and confidence. He was and always will be a part of my Girlfriend Network.

After the move to Tulsa, I also gained a new guy Girlfriend. His name? Chris. While anchoring the five o'clock evening news, I had the pleasure of working in our Special Projects unit doing investigations. One of the folks I worked closely with was Chris.

Mind you, we were oil and water for a couple of years. But after he and his girlfriend at the time broke up, he showed up on my porch heartbroken that she'd gone out with someone else. (Since Chris and I were not good friends at the time, I truly think it was a God thing that he turned to me for help.) Chris ended up hanging out with my husband, our new baby and me all weekend to lick his wounds.

Amy & Chris w/ Todd & me vacationing in Chicago

That's when I saw a new side to this tough-as-nails co-worker. He opened up, and I began to trust what I saw. I actually ended up calling his girlfriend (after I was sure he was serious about taking their relationship to the next step) and convinced her to see him again. Now Chris and Amy are married with a precious daughter, Avery. (I'm grinning ear to ear just typing that!) Needless to say, after he showed up on my front porch, our relationship at work and away from work changed dramatically. Chris and I helped each other succeed, problem solve, and laugh. Yep, like Mick, he became a trusted part of my Girlfriend network.

As luck would have it, Chris and I spent years ramping up the investigative unit at the station—Chris as the producer and me as the reporter. And boy, did we have some wild times! There was the time we were investigating prostitutes advertising on the Internet. (Who knew they offered lunchtime specials?!) So Chris, a photographer, and I hid in a tiny shower together, waiting for our pretend "John" to reveal he was really part of a TV news crew. Looking back on that, I have two thoughts: 1) Did we really do that story? 2) Thank goodness none of those women of the evening were packing heat!

Then there was the stake-out at a swingers' bar for a story on the fact that the Bible Belt does have a little-known

Winning awards with Chris (left) and photojournalist Richard (on right)

seedy underside. (If you don't know what a swingers' bar is, God bless you. Ignorance is bliss, and certain images are unfortunately stamped into my brain for a lifetime because of that story!) But of course, not all our investigations were so tabloid-ish (which equaled ratings); Chris and I actually had a great synergy that turned into award-winning investigations and we actually made a difference in our community.

To this day, though, it makes me sad when someone looks at me like I've grown three heads after mentioning that Chris is one of my Girlfriends. Seriously, broaden your horizons, folks! I enjoy talking with him and getting a different perspective on things. We've helped each other through work issues, fertility problems, and layoffs. Chris was in the first round of layoffs at the station. That broke my heart. Then, when I found out I might be laid off, I called him...often. (Who would understand my fears better than someone who'd just faced them?) I find it interesting that some coworkers only believe we were "friends" because of work, and yet we ended up being better friends in spite of it.

*Mark, Michelle, Todd & me @
an event we emceed*

I have so many wonderful Guyfriends because I opened up the possibility that extremely special men would make my Support Network so much richer. My co-anchor for the last twelve years, Mark, has been such a bonus in my life. I call him my "TV Husband" because I often saw him more hours a day than my real husband, and I put complete faith in him on live TV for 1,560 hours of my life. (That's a guesstimation of a thirty-minute newscast, five days a week, for a dozen years. Yes, it's official; I'm a research nerd!) Anyhoo, not only have Mark and I worked so well together on the anchor desk, he's someone I've always been able to talk with. He's a good Christian man with a precious family, and I'm lucky to be such great friends with him.

Rick & me

And then there have been valuable Guyfriends outside of work. Rick and I laugh that we go way back to the days when we were both super duper skinny and had lots of hair (mine was long and his was actually on his head). When I was Miss Collinsville during college and getting ready for Miss Oklahoma, I lived for a couple of months with the pageant director, who just happened to be Rick's mother. He ended up coming home that summer to take a break from his producing position at the "Sally Jesse Raphael Show." We've been fast friends ever since and he always makes me laugh! Rick has been an expert at re-invention during his life—from tabloid TV, to ministry, to speaking all over the country. He's like a cat with nine lives, and each one of them is amazing and successful. So he became not just a friend, but a source of wisdom after I learned I might be laid off.

And I can't forget Jay, who has shopped, cried, and giggled with me at all times of the day and night. Not only has he done my hair for years, he's gone above and beyond the call of duty. What hairdresser do you know who will touch up roots (shhhhh!) at midnight because that was the only time we both had free? But our bond is more than that. We've definitely been through sickness and health together, holding hands the whole way. He knows some of my best-kept secrets and I know his. We are two peas in a pod, and I'm lucky to have him in my inner circle!

Jay who is my friend & amazing hairdresser

So, you can see the opposite sex can be very valuable in the Friend department. But trust your senses and instincts. If a guy wants more than a totally platonic friendship, keep him at arm's length. I will tell you, there are two guys over the years that I started to bring into my "inner circle," and my hubby put his foot down. While he's used to my Guyfriends, he just felt these guys had more up their sleeve than being best buds. You know what? I trusted his instinct. Over the years, he has become a big believer in my diverse friend base, so if he feels something's not right, I think I'm wise to trust that. Looking back, I think Todd was totally right about those two guys. Believe me, you need to have a good, strong and trusting marriage to have really close Guyfriends. But if you have "buy in" from your spouse (if you're married), you will have a much richer life because of it.

Todd & Me on our honeymoon

Here's where I feel like I need to give a shout-out to my sweet hubby. He is quite a keeper for someone who I met at "Penny Beer Night." (Oops...did I really say that out loud?) Now, not to make it sound like I'd go home with any guy in a bar (which I would not!), Todd did come into the hangout with all his pledge brothers, whom I knew quite well. It just so happened I was there with several of my Miss Oklahoma pageant friends and sorority sisters so, of course, these guys were drawn to us. (Funny how, at the time, I thought these guys I knew just came over to say "hi" to me. Ha!) However, the one guy I didn't know (who was sooo cute) asked me to dance, and the rest is history. I knew within three months he was the man I wanted to marry. Todd was (and is) the most incredible combination of chemistry and being my absolute best Guyfriend.

You may or may not have picked a good one with your spouse (if you're married), but I hit the jackpot! Maybe I picked him like I pick my Girlfriends, or maybe it's a God thing (who knew someone would say "Penny Beer Night" was a godsend?),

W/ Todd @ the ballpark

but Todd "gets" me and I'm the one reaping the rewards. Todd understands that I have Girlfriends and Guyfriends. He supports me no matter what. He may goof up (who doesn't?), but he's the first to say he's sorry (me too!). Next to my father, Todd Morrison is the best man I've ever met in my life. He doesn't complain about doing the laundry, he's never made me feel bad about not being a cook, and he's sexy as heck! I love my hubby more now than the day we married. Is that because I married my best Guyfriend (with benefits) or because I'm just lucky? I can't answer that. If I had married the guy I dated most of my college years (which I would have, if he'd asked), I would have ended up a farmer's wife in a small Oklahoma town. I'm not saying that's a bad gig, it's just not me! (Hello? Can we say Green Acres? Stilettos and cow patties are not a good combo!) But I'd grown up quite a bit by the time I met Todd, and it was kismet. Pick well, my Girlfriends. Guyfriends are the new Girlfriend, and your hubby better be one of them.

Here's your sixth Girlfriends Challenge:

1. Don't pick your Girlfriends on gender alone, because you'll be missing out on a different perspective and knowledge base.

2. Make sure you only bring those exceptional guys into your inner circle who are completely trustworthy and are only platonic friends. (In other words, don't ruin it for the rest of us by having some fling with a "Guyfriend," because then we're left to constantly justify our Guyfriends.)

3. I challenge you to expand your Friendship Network to the best people possible!

CHAPTER 7

Seriously?...

My mother and father have given me great advice. How could they not? My mother is my original Girlfriend, and my father, as a psychologist, gives advice for a living. But since leaving home, I have gotten some of my best life lessons from my Girlfriends. You know what I'm talking about—those epiphanies that leave you saying, "Seriously? It's so simple and yet I never thought of that!" Some of this advice is about frivolous things like style (as you've read about in previous chapters), but the most life-changing things have been about growing up (remember my bridesmaids?) and, more recently, marriage and raising children. See? Surround yourself by "10s," and that advice will be better than most therapy sessions and a heck of a lot cheaper.

My wonderful mom & dad on a cruise

My Girlfriend Sue is the closest thing I've ever had to a sister. Yes, she's one of my fashion sistas, but she's also a very wise woman who has lived through her share of heartaches. Yet nothing ever gets her down. She has had diabetes since she was a little girl, suffered two heart attacks, and then a horse fell on her in Colorado, which required doctors to rebuild her face with titanium. (Although we have laughed that the horse accident will cut down on Botox later!) Seriously, Sue has suffered some major blows and, yet, her sunny attitude never wavers. That has been a life lesson for me in itself, but, with her wise advice, she has also changed the way I parent.

Sue (right) with her daughter Ashley (left) and my daughter Marlowe (center)

Todd and I had our kids a little later in life. We were both enjoying our careers and marriage so our first child, Peyton, was a surprise after eight years of wedded bliss. Sure, we're some of the older parents in PTA meetings, but the upside is that many of my friends can pass along their "been there, done that" advice. Sue is a perfect example, because her children are about ten years older than mine (which has always made her daughter, Ashley, the perfect age to babysit!).

While Sue has passed along a lot of motherly advice, one thing has always stuck with me: "It's easy to be a bad parent, but it's hard to be good one." Wiser words about parenting have never been spoken.

You see, our son, Peyton, was a handful until the age of four. Even my baby-proofing at the house had to be baby-proofed around that child. I'm not kidding! Peyton liked to fingerpaint with his poop, climb anything that appeared to be off limits, and push his mama (yeah...me!) to the brink of insanity. There were no "family" dinners out because Peyton could clear a restaurant within ten minutes with his fits. (Even now, just remembering me trying to take him anywhere civilized during that phase sends shivers down my spine.) But, where I saw the end of my rope, "Aunt Sue" saw the beauty of raising a child who was all boy. When I wanted to take the easy way out (never leaving the house), Sue saw the opportunity to mold a child who was driven, and she was right. It would have been so much easier to throw up my hands and hire a sitter all the time. Instead, she reminded me that being a good parent

Todd holding Peyton "Then"

Me with Peyton "Now"

is not always easy. I'm so glad she helped me through that thought process (and Peyton's wild man phase), because whatever I let him get away with at that age would have only become worse with time. Instead, she encouraged me to take Peyton on boy-friendly outings to let him release some of that energy. If Todd and I needed a "date night," her daughter Ashley would babysit, with Sue always willing to lend some relief when he became too much of a handful. And you know what? The wild child phase finally ended, and I have an incredible kid! Decisions and parenting still aren't always easy, but that very difficult time showed me that "this too shall pass." Just do what you can to be the best parent you can be. There's no owner's manual when it comes to children, so you really need to depend on your friends to help you through those tough decisions and not take the easy way out. Sue definitely talked me off the ceiling more than once and reminded me to get back to the basics of what matters most—raising kids to become responsible adults. What a concept! Being a good parent is hard, but we can do it with a little help from our friends. These days it truly does take a village to raise a family.

On a side note—I have a hilarious story about Sue and Peyton. (Okay, I'm rolling on the floor laughing so hard. I'm not sure I can actually type it—but I'll try....) We used to take Peyton to the pool and hang out at the baby pool area. Usually, it was just the three of us—Peyton, Sue, and me. But on one particular day, the baby pool was suddenly crowded with 30- and 40-somethings. I was baffled, but Sue decided it was because they wanted to meet "Cindy—the TV broadcaster." (Gulp! Does it have to be when I'm in a bathing suit?) Whether that was the case is beside the point (but you can see how your identity might get caught up in this whole celebrity status thing). The point is, there were a lot of ladies hanging with us, so I suddenly felt the need to suck in my tummy a bit more.

You should know, Peyton has always had a thing for sports. His first "security blanket" was a rubber OU football, "ball" was his first word, and the kid could throw a spiral at eighteen months. (Hello? It is Oklahoma...the land of football. Can I hear a BOOMER...oh, sorry! I'll get back to the story.) It goes without saying that Peyton was in the baby pool with every kind of ball you can imagine. All the ladies would squeal with delight and clap when Peyton threw a ball out of the pool. (Yeah...precious. Whatever! That meant I had to get up and prance in my bathing suit to go get the dang thing! Argh!) Anyway, Peyton finally had the idea to throw out as many balls as possible all at once to see Mommy scramble. When all the balls went flying, I finally called "uncle." No more prancing, no more staring, no more balls! That's when Peyton proceeded to throw the fit of all fits, so Aunt Sue stood up and announced to the group, "Well, a man can never have enough balls!" Then she took off after all the balls while I tried to keep my son from drowning during his little stunt. Needless to say, everyone (except my son, of course) grew completely quiet. When Sue finally returned to her seat beside me on the edge of the baby pool, she leaned over and whispered to me, "Did I really just say loudly that a man can never have too many balls?" Yes...yes, you did, Sue. And because it was true, we suddenly doubled over in a fit of giggles. We laughed so hard even my son started laughing. Oh my goodness, we laughed and laughed and laughed. Slowly but surely, we ended up with the baby pool to ourselves once again, and Sue and I took great pleasure in knowing we had no shame, and men can never have enough balls.

Mignon and Me in Vegas

Another great piece of advice was from my Girlfriend Mignon. You see, Minnie has four boys who are four years and four months apart. (Better her than me, that's for sure!) If there's anyone who can whip that motley crew into shape, it is Mignon. During one of our Glamour Girl vacays to Vegas, Mignon said something profound: "You should never become a Martyr Mom." This was something I'd never heard of...what's that? Mignon went on to tell me about the Martyr Moms she'd met who had given up everything for their kids...and, boy, were they bitter. We're not talking about the wonderful moms who give up their career to raise children or the moms who sacrifice nice things for their children. No, these are moms who talk non-stop about what they've given up to provide their children everything. These moms complain they have no life (and make sure they don't have a life) because of their kids. There is no reason moms and kids can't co-exist together. Are you going to sacrifice things for your child? Absolutely! We all do that, Girlfriend. The thing we don't do is complain all the dang time about it.

Mignon reminded me that even the best wives and mothers have their own lives. They do something for themselves. Remember when I talked about the cup in a previous chapter? If you don't fill your cup, no one else may do it. And that's a thirsty existence. Instead, make sure you occasionally fill your cup up with your hopes, dreams, and needs. Don't whine about your "mother" obligations. Instead, hire the occasional babysitter so you can have some girlfriend time, or start a hobby. There's no reason to put your life totally on hold until your kids fly the coop to live on their own. As my mom always says, you better keep up your marriage during the kid phase because it's just the two of you again when the kids leave. I guess the same applies to us as women. If you know who you are and have a life besides being a mom, then the transition might not be so tough during those empty nest years.

My Girlfriend Michelle is married to my former Tulsa co-anchor, Mark. She's a hoot and definitely "lives in the moment." She's constantly reminding me that "life is too short." And you know what? She's right. Life is too short to do a job you don't like, be around people who bring

Michelle & me @ a station Christmas party

you down, and spend time sweating the small stuff. Whenever I want to hear how to live a carefree life, or be reminded I'm taking things too seriously, I call Michelle. We all have "issues" and worries, but we shouldn't spend all our life stressing. Instead, enjoy life here and now and don't forget to laugh.

Why is Michelle so naturally carefree? Well, first of all, she's a 40-something trapped in the body of a 20-year-old (hate her!). But it's more than her looks because she actually acts like she found the Fountain of Youth. She doesn't spend time dwelling on mistakes in the past or worrying about what could happen in the future. Instead, she enjoys laughing at what's happening now and living for today. And you know what? That doesn't just keep *her* young, but it has the same effect on her husband (and my former Tulsa TV hubby) Mark. He's ten years older than Michelle and is very methodical, responsible and mature (all good qualities for a newscaster and man of the house). But whenever he gets too serious or worried, Michelle brings him back to the moment. Her attitude is infectious and keeps everyone around her hip, young and happy, no matter their age. (After all, age *is* just a number.) So, try living in the moment and see if you don't feel better.

Two of my best Girlfriends (who happen to be guys) have also given me handy, dandy life tips that have made such a difference. I told you about my former Oklahoma City co-anchor, Mick. He's one sharp cookie. Well, when I found out I might be getting laid off, I called Mick, crying. (Once again, God bless those really close male friends in my life!) The advice he gave me on that first phone call was huge. "Rarely do people get out of TV when they want to." Jackpot! Mick reminded me that ratings, a management whim, or the timing of a contract are all out of an anchor's control. All you can do is do your best. The rest is out of your hands, so don't beat yourself up over it.

Mick reminded me that I had done nothing wrong...sometimes life just happens. I think you can look at the state of the economy right now, and you can probably relate. In our changing times, many careers besides the fickle TV news business, are in the same boat. I can't do anything about advertisers deciding to cut back on TV ads because money is tight,

Mick (Mayor of OKC)

just like a widget guy can't do anything about customers deciding not to buy widgets because it's not a necessity right now. You can give 110%, but reality is reality. That is the point where you need to decide if you're going to be a victim or survivor. In other words, it's okay to feel helpless, but don't become hopeless. Helpless means you can find strength and peace when you ask for and receive help. Hopeless means there is no hope. Mick helped me to realize I was only helpless, and the strength of my support network could and would help me survive this big bump in the road.

Mick didn't just remind me of that during the one phone conversation. Since then, Mick has called or texted me weekly to see how I'm doing, ask if I need help with anything, and encourage me to not just survive, but to thrive. So, while most folks may not choose to be laid off, they can choose to be happy, healthy, and full of hope...especially with a little help from their friends. Thank you, Mick.

One of my favorite sayings in life is, "When you find yourself in a hole, stop digging." Well, my friend Chris took that a

Chris with his wife Amy & baby Avery

step further by saying, "It's one thing to dig yourself into a hole... it's another to hand someone a shovel to help you." He's right. Sometimes you can't always see the hole until you're in it, so be very careful who you invite to help bury you.

As I mentioned earlier, it wasn't until my 40s that I really learned to dump the wanna-bes. Before that, I was much more trusting and often took in any "friend" who came my way. That drove Chris crazy! With my rather public career, Chris believes I'm flypaper for the wanna-bes. And while it's not a bad thing to "never meet a stranger," you also need to make sure those folks you let close only have your best interests at heart. Many a time Chris would warn me about handing a shovel to someone—heck, I'd practically beg them to help me dig!—only to be disappointed they didn't really care about me.

That was certainly the case with the gal who eventually became my Suzie Sabotage. Chris warned me that she had a rep for running over folks. He said much the same thing about my Competitive Cathy. Sure enough, both tried to bury me when given the chance. Shame on them for that kind of behavior, but more importantly, shame on me that I handed them the shovel. It's just a good thing I've surrounded myself with Girlfriends like Chris who have my back and have always thrown me a rope to crawl out of the hole.

Before I go any further, let's recap some of the great advice I've gotten that might help you as well, because any true Girlfriend is going to pass along the good stuff:

- It's easy to be a bad parent but it's hard to be a good one. (I remember this one daily!)

- You should never become a Martyr Mom. (Try to work toward a good life balance—besides your Girlfriends are tired of listening to your complaints!)

- Live in the moment. (Don't spend all your time wishing for "shoulda," "woulda," "coulda" but instead, rejoice and enjoy all the blessings you have today.)

- Rarely do people get out of TV when they want to. (What does that mean for you? Sometimes life happens beyond your control, but it's up to you to become a survivor, not a victim.)

- It's one thing to dig yourself into a hole...it's another to hand someone a shovel to help you. (Dump the wanna-bes, and certainly don't invite them to bury you.)

The list of my wise (beyond their years) Girlfriends goes on and on. Sometimes the advice they give isn't always groundbreaking, but that doesn't mean it's not life-changing. For instance, my Mexico trip was full of advice that affects me to this day. How many times have I valued an evening with my Girlfriends Cindy, Jill, DC, or Tiffany when we have talked through, and solved, the problems of the moment? Surround yourself with people who are willing to share life's secrets to happiness and other tidbits that leave you saying, "Seriously? That's brilliant!"

Here's your seventh Girlfriends Challenge:

1. Jot down a list of some of the best advice your Girlfriends have given you. You'll be surprised at the insight you'll gain.

2. Surround yourself only with Girlfriends who have no agendas but instead want to pass along tidbits (large and small) that make a difference in your life.

3. Make sure you keep the inspiration chain going by passing along your own words of wisdom that you've learned, either on your own or from your Girlfriend Network.

CHAPTER 8

*Thank God you love me...
in spite of me.*

Let's face it...everyone goofs up. But it is only your *real* Girlfriends who will forgive you, counsel you, and maybe even pretend it never happened. Now this isn't going to be a long chapter because my mother is not only going to read this book, but give it to all her Girlfriends. While my Girlfriends might forgive me for some of my "whoppers," my mother might never live them down. So, just as I protected the names of the guilty in Chapter Two, so I shall save face and not confess all my sins here.

Hypothetically, there might have been a summer that a certain TV anchor was having difficulties dealing with her job. Remember the end-of-summer Mexico trip where I...ummm, that TV person... found out a lot about herself and how she wasn't totally identified by her job?

Well, before the epiphany during that vacay, she spent much of the summer consuming more than her fair share of adult beverages. Oh, heck...this is way too complicated. Forget the hypothetical! I was dealing badly with the pressure, fear of failure, and not reaching that ten o'clock evening anchor "goal." (Sorry, Mom, I gotta fess up!) Anyway, one holiday at the lake I became very withdrawn (totally not me!) and simply indulged in more wine than I should have. There...I said it! Do you know the worst part? My family and two other dear families saw the train wreck (ugh!).

Okay...I need to take a deep breath here and clear the tears from my eyes. That last paragraph was a tough one. Maybe this should have been the memoir where I could do no wrong, but that's not real life. We all have issues, problems, and cracks in the façade. We all make mistakes, say things we shouldn't, and do things we wish we could take back. I guess that's why they say we live and learn. Now, I'll go back to falling on my sword....

My precious friends, Sue and Chris, watched their Girlfriend become distant and pretty much fall apart on that lake holiday weekend, but they didn't spend the weekend talking in hushed tones or taking notes so they could throw me under the bus when we got back to Tulsa. What did they do instead? They loved me in spite of me. Each of them sat and had a long talk with me about what they saw, why they were worried, and where we needed to go from there. The talks weren't necessarily pretty, but both of my Friends were respectful, kind, and helpful. They helped me realize a lot. First of all, we determined I was somewhat depressed and probably needed to ask for some professional help. (Since I have a psychologist as a father, I thought that was a pretty great idea.)

Secondly, we talked about the drinking. There were no judgments, only support. They helped me to realize a lot—mainly that I needed to get my act together. And you know what? They were right. Only a true Girlfriend would realize I wasn't really in crisis mode, but instead needed an attitude adjustment. It wasn't a time to turn away, but a time to love and help me. I owe them a lot for that.

Unfortunately, that's not the only time I've done or said things I wish I hadn't (shocker!). In fact, if I thought about it hard enough, this could probably be the longest chapter just highlighting all my "goofs." While I'm by no means an emotional vampire or serial offender, I can quite confidently say that I've probably disappointed or hurt each of my Girlfriends at one time or another. The fact is, if you are Girlfriends long enough, it's bound to happen. The difference is, Girlfriends know their love and caring is real and runs deep. We're all human and no one's perfect. Luckily, there's plenty of room in the Girlfriends Network for forgiveness all the way around—your Girlfriends forgive you and you forgive yourself.

Chris, Sue & Todd have all loved me in spite of me

That brings up another point. When you're with your Girlfriends, you shouldn't feel like you're walking on eggshells or that you have to edit everything you say. True Friendship is about being you, growing and living life, and on that very rare occasion when someone gets hurt feelings, it shouldn't become a big drama because your Girlfriends know you would never knowingly hurt them. But what if boundaries have been crossed? It's time to be gently honest about it. There's no guilt or finger-pointing, but instead the conversation comes from a place of love and respect. Mistakes happen, but the only way to truly clean the slate is to forgive and then to forget.

There's also plenty of room in your Girlfriend relationships to agree to disagree. My Girlfriend, Sue, and I are living proof of that one. We agree on most of the big things, but occasionally we disagree on something about which we're passionate. Oh sure, we may try to convince the other about why one is right (me) and the other might be misled (Sue). However, at the end of the day, we just agree to respect each other. Aretha Franklin was spot on when she sang about "R-E-S-P-E-C-T." It is a must between Girlfriends. With respect you can agree to disagree on some things *and* help guide a Girlfriend who may have lost her way.

Here's your eighth Girlfriends Challenge:

1. You love your Girlfriends in spite of their occasional mistakes just as they love you in spite of yours — because (unfortunately) no one is perfect.

2. If a Girlfriend loses her way, be there to help and guide her, not to talk about her in hushed tones behind her back.

3. Being a Girlfriend is not about winning or being right, it's about respect and love.

Hosting telethon almost 20 years ago

KOCO pic early in my career

Covering OKC bombing in 1995

w/ Helicopter pilot in OKC

Reporting live in the 90s

Emceeing event w/ Tulsa co-anchor Mark

w/ Helicopter pilot in Tulsa during appearance

CHAPTER 9

Didn't you used to be somebody?

At the beginning of this book, I told you I'd never forget the words my news director told me: "We don't know if we can renew your contract. It depends on the economy." That conversation took place January of 2009. I was lost, alone, and afraid. My fear was not just because I wondered how I was going to help provide for my family, but also because I was afraid of losing myself. Who was I really? Cindy...Emmy-winning anchor and investigative reporter. That's how I've introduced myself for years. Suddenly I knew life was about to change drastically, and I had better reinvent myself. However, I was so blindsided that I was frozen with fear. About the only thing I could do at the time was cry. I had nightmares, night after night, that I'd be somewhere and someone would ask, "You look familiar...didn't you used to be on TV?" In other words,

"Didn't you used to be *somebody*?" It's a statement that makes any has-been TV anchor's blood run cold.

Instead of focusing on being a Has-Been before it even happened (read: Cindy in the fetal position for five months), my Girlfriends spent every bit of that time putting me back together again, piece by piece. From the Support Network that I had formed (see Chapters One through Eight), I had help in every part of my life. First up to bat came my closest friends, known as the Inner Circle. They're the ones who just let me cry and cry and cry. They helped me grieve my possible loss and express my fears. Things I couldn't say to my husband because I didn't want him to worry ("Can I do anything else?" or "Am I a loser?!"), I was able to openly say (more than once) to my Inner Circle. Girlfriends (and Guyfriends) Cindy, Sue, Chris, DC, Mick, and a handful of others got an earful, and yet they never denied me a shoulder to cry on or a midnight phone call.

Sue, Amy, Chris & Todd @ Peyton's School Play

I can't stress how important it is to have that Inner Circle. I don't know what I would have done without them. They put me back together like Humpty Dumpty and kept me going for me, my family, and my future. When I thought I couldn't show up another day at the station and read a story about another layoff, (yes, my heart broke each time I talked about "downsizing" on the news), my Girlfriends convinced me I could do it...one day at a time. Unfortunately, my daily heartbreak was about more than just putting on a front for viewers during a thirty-minute newscast. You see, none of my co-workers knew my situation (except my co-anchor Mark), so I had to act like nothing was wrong at work for months, on and off the news set.

Once my Inner Circle made sure I was mentally stable (good luck with that one!), the next round of wonderful Girlfriends came in to do their work. As I told you at the beginning of this book, I felt very safe being part of the corporate flock—pay me every two weeks, take out my 401k, and sign me to a new contract every three years. (Bah!) In return, this little sheep was as loyal as they come. But when it became evident (in my case, at least) that Corporate America was hungry for lamb chops, my Girlfriends knew they had to help me change my mindset. They knew my loyalty, in this day and age, needed to be to myself and my family, not a business. And although I'd never set foot in the business school at OU, they understood I needed to believe I could be a successful businesswoman. The whole time, my Girlfriends were not swayed by my whimpers. Instead they nudged, coaxed, and pushed me away from the herd and over the fence to freedom.

This is where some old Girlfriends 1.0 version wouldn't have worked. My Girlfriends didn't say "Get a job! Any job! And quit whining." That would have certainly been the easy way out. Nope, instead they helped me to look within myself, to explore my passions and find my calling. (And no...shoe shopping did not count!) My Girlfriend Carol had already laid the groundwork for me to start my own business when we were on vacay several years ago in Mexico. While she didn't push the issue then, she kicked things into overdrive at the idea I might get laid off. She showed me what to do and how to do it, at which point I formed my own LLC—limited liability corporation (ooh, such big words!).

I'll never forget the late night phone calls I had with my Guyfriend Rick. I mentioned earlier (in the Guyfriends chapter) that Rick has brilliantly and successfully reinvented himself more times than a cat has lives. It was nothing short of sheer brilliance when he suggested that I write a book and hit the speaking circuit since I was a speaker and writer by nature. What a novel idea (sorry for the pun)! He hit the nail on the head with that one. That's what I know, what I'm passionate about, and what I've won awards for doing! What would I speak or write about? Argh! Details....

The topic, however, quickly became crystal clear. When I needed to file a trade mark, Friends Stuart and Tiffany lent their legal expertise. When I began to wonder what my hourly rate would be, my Girlfriends Melanie and Deedra came up with a formula. When I worried if anyone would buy a book based on my ideas, my Girlfriend Donna made me promise the first signing would be at her boutique. My Girlfriend Jill offered to take new pictures that weren't so TV-ish. (That's the picture on the cover!) More and more Girlfriends came to my rescue with ideas and support. The book became a no-brainer. I needed to help women build a Support Network like mine to not just survive, but to thrive. I was living proof the Girlfriends Network was alive and well, and if you surround yourself with wonderful people, you will be able to make it through anything. "Girlfriends 2.0" was born!

By day, I worked at the station and anchored the five o'clock evening news like nothing was wrong. At night and on the weekends, I was pondering my book. At one point I asked my Girlfriend Julie (a psychologist) for the best advice I could give women to empower them. She came up with a simple,

Anchoring the 5 o'clock news

yet perfect, analogy. "Your Girlfriends should be like your board of directors." Hmmm...that's an interesting concept and right on target. Every successful non-profit has a board of directors. These people all have a common passion and help the organization with fundraisers, marketing, programs, and any other facet the charity needs to stay afloat and on course. Each board member brings his or her own expertise, and your Girlfriends are much the same. For instance, I'm at one end of my board of director's table, and my husband is at the other. Seated along either side are Girlfriends (and Guyfriends) who keep me balanced, successful, and happy in every aspect of my life. My Inner Circle works almost like my executive board because they are the Friends who are the most passionate advisers, have the closest bond, and have the biggest investment. Other board members seated at the table are ones who keep me in check with children, husband, job, attitude, and just about everything else in my life. They all have their own expertise that makes me a better person.

While my board of directors was keeping me sane and setting my sails in the right direction, we couldn't do it alone. I needed a little more help, and it was time to call in the cavalry. That's when I decided I needed to step outside my comfort zone and find new Friends who wouldn't actually sit on my board but would still help guide me in this brave, new world. Think of it this way: even the best non-profit can't survive on its board of directors alone. It often needs volunteers to help with a fundraiser or to fulfill a mission statement. And you know what? You can find Friends in the darnedest places!

Since I wanted to hit the speaking circuit, I joined the National Speakers Association and attended the Oklahoma chapter meeting. I didn't know a soul in the room. While I'm not shy, and I'm certainly not worried about hitting places alone (I'm an only child for goodness sakes), I was quite intimidated by going to a new organization and learning, meeting, and proving myself all over again. I had "been there, done that" in the TV news world. I had gone to the IRE (Investigative Reporters and Editors) conventions alone. No biggie. It's all the same people, for the most part, year after year. Plus, that world was my life. Now, suddenly, I was forcing myself into a new place with new people, talking about a subject I didn't know. (Shoot me now!)

I got the guts to go to my first National Speakers Association Oklahoma meeting in April. When we went around the room introducing ourselves, I confessed for the first time publicly that I might be facing a layoff and was looking at a career change. My palms were sweating as I talked, and normally I never get nervous speaking to a crowd. But talking about my reinvention out loud, in front of strangers, made it sound so real. (Gulp!) After I sat down, a man slipped me his card with a note attached. Basically, it said if I wanted to hit the speaking circuit, I was in a perfect place to do so because of my experience in the media. Whew! I had a friend! Even more importantly, I soon learned the card and note came from one of the top speakers in the business—a man

W/ Dr. Jeff Magee

named Jeff Magee. Jeff and I met off and on for months as he began helping me formulate my new career. He definitely paid it forward by teaching me about databases, sharing his marketing ideas, and introducing me to speakers' bureaus. He certainly didn't have to help me, but he did it gladly. Jeff has definitely become a Friend... one I wouldn't have found if I hadn't been looking.

I found more new Friends by just opening my eyes. While talking on Twitter with social media experts about reinvention, I met a brander out of Detroit named Hajj. He helped me retool my branding. For those of you who don't know what branding is, let me give you insight because that has been a huge part of my reinvention. Branding is basically your reputation—what you put online, write or talk about, or how you present yourself. Branding can shape how others see you. Make sense? Pretty cool, huh? It's elementary and, yet, so crucial to business these days. As this book goes to print, Hajj and I still haven't met in person, but we still talk on the phone and exchange ideas. Funny how 140 characters on something with as silly a name as Twitter ended up making a connection which in turn made such a difference in my life. Now that is truly reading between the lines!

Who would guess I'd also get some valuable advice from someone I hadn't seen since high school? One of my classmates, Mark, grew from a smart and dedicated student in the 80s to a polished and highly successful business professor. It turns out, Mark had been following my "life changes" on Facebook (gotta love social media!) and offered to give me some advice on pinpointing my business niche. (Business has a niche?) So, during our high school reunion last summer, we talked at length about not getting caught up in the small things that were driving me crazy. He also helped me focus on what I needed to do and the difference I wanted to make in the world. I gladly gobbled up any and all advice Mark gave me and we've even discussed a joint project in the future.

See? When you've learned to spot the wanna-bes (danger, Will Robinson!), and you're not asking someone to sit on your Board of Directors (that's a big responsibility), then you'll find all kinds of Friends/Girlfriends who can help you grow, learn, and be a better person.

So, as the months passed, my Girlfriends (both my core Board of Directors and my new Friends drifting in and out) helped me feel more relaxed, stronger, and excited at the prospect of a new career. Now that's not to say I wanted to leave the station...oh, no! I still wanted to stay there and work through at least two face lifts (if you think I'm kidding, I'm not!). And while my Girlfriends prepared me as much as possible for a layoff, they also gave me another gift. You see, it was very easy to become bitter at my station. (Why me?

I was loyal!) However, as my Girlfriends reminded me, many of my new opportunities were possible because of the twelve years I'd spent at the station. I had built up a following that might enjoy reading a book I had written. I'd won national awards there that had built my reputation, and I'd grown as a person, journalist, wife, and mother (both of my kids were born in Tulsa while I worked at the station). Almost like not letting go of the emotional ties of Suzie Sabotage, my Girlfriends helped me realize that being bitter at the station would have only poisoned me and wasted my energy.

I'd spent four months reconciling how I felt about the station, realizing I was more than my job, and carving a new path just in case I was laid off. By mid May (less than two months before my contract expired), I was scared but prepared to learn my fate. Sure enough, that day came mid-month. My general manager and news director called me into a meeting. I was prepared for almost anything, because it's fairly common for a station to tell you you're done, send you home, and then your personal items arrive in boxes at your home the next day. I only hoped things would go better for me than all the other station employees who'd been laid off in the months before.

The meeting was brief but friendly. The bottom line? The station couldn't afford me. They would not be renewing my contract—it was official. I stifled the lump that came to my throat (that was so different than January when the mere thought I might lose my job sent me into soap opera-worthy tears). Still, I had to ask, "Have I done anything wrong? Is there anything I can change? Anything I can do?"

"No. It is what it is."

I guess those words from my general manager summed it up. It was the economy—nothing more, nothing less. I could be sad...I could be mad...I could scream. Nothing would make it better. Starting July first, I would have no job and no income.

I left the meeting feeling numb, but in a different way than I did in January. Back then I felt helpless. Who am I? What do I do? Can I do anything else? (Mommy, make the boo-boo go away!) After this meeting, I felt like my course was charted and it was time to set sail, like it or not. I let some co-workers know (I was tired of feeling like I was living a lie), and I put a statement out on social media. It was out in the open. (I just didn't have it in me anymore to pretend I was part of the Stepford family.) I was disappointed, but I had a new purpose. I was sad, but I felt excited at the new opportunities. I was lost, and yet I felt free. I loved my twelve years at the station with all my heart, but it was time to move on and accept the inevitable. My Girlfriends prepared me as much as possible to say "goodbye" to TV news, and "hello" to a whole new world.

Now I had less than two months to enjoy what was definitely the end of my job and maybe (sniff!) even the end of a stellar career. Might there be another TV job? Absolutely! I hope so! I'm not totally ready to let that dream go because I absolutely love TV news. But pretty much every station in the country is hurting from the lack of viewers, the popularity of news on the Internet, and the economy. Hiring freezes, pay cuts, layoffs, and furloughs are a way of life in TV news right now.

I had built my reputation in TV and I'd stayed fiercely loyal to the station for 12 years, but now it was time for me to have a new loyalty. It was time to build a new future for me and my family. In the meantime, I decided to soak in each and every moment of anchoring with Mark, turning a story that makes a difference for someone, and enjoying the buzz of a newsroom.

By the way, this was *supposed* to be my last chapter. I was going to ride off into the sunset with my family and Girlfriends for richer pastures (literally, I hoped!). Guess I should have put my head on a swivel and run a zig-zag pattern because, unfortunately, life had other plans. But, before we move on...let's do what has become a tradition and let's talk Girlfriend challenges.

Here's your ninth Girfriends Challenge:

1. Make sure you know your Inner Circle—those you can trust with your deepest secrets and who will help you no matter how rough the road.

2. Make sure you create a board of directors who will help you and make sure you succeed in every aspect of your life.

3. Stretch past your comfort zone to find Fringe Friends who can help you in areas you may never have needed help before.

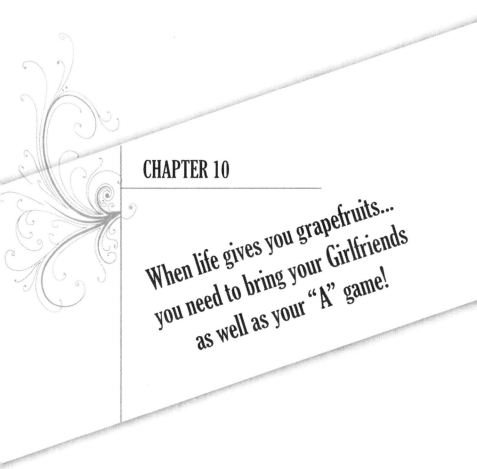

CHAPTER 10

When life gives you grapefruits...
you need to bring your Girlfriends
as well as your "A" game!

Two weeks after learning the station could no longer afford me, my stomach began to hurt one morning while I was putting on my makeup. It hurt worse than childbirth! Suddenly, I was doubled over and throwing up. What the heck? My husband (wisely) decided to rush me to the emergency room, but I remember telling him it must be stress. In fact, once we got to the ER, my symptoms went away. (Argh...it's like the car that acts up until you take to the mechanic!) But since we were there, my frightened husband insisted on staying (whatever!). Oh, how I love that man, because while waiting for a doctor in the exam room, I had another attack. It was worse than the first time. They gave me morphine (ahhhh...), then ran every test imaginable.

I was prepared to be told I was a head case (uh, stress much?). I was even ready to be told I had a kidney stone or my appendix had burst. I was speechless and totally unprepared when the ER doctor came back into the room and prepared me for a vaginal exam (just one more reason this is a Girlfriends' book!). I was suddenly in panic mode when he mentioned a tumor. My grandmother died from ovarian cancer! First my job...now this? Yep, a CAT scan proved there was a substantial-sized tumor that had to be removed. I was stunned. If a layoff wasn't a part of my master plan, you can bet that cancer definitely wasn't!

I spent the next couple of days with my internist and the top ovarian cancer specialist in the area. It turns out that the substantial tumor was actually the size of a grapefruit! What? Holy Hannah! Once again, I had to return to work and go back on the air as if nothing was wrong. Well, let's see...something *was* wrong because I was losing my job (the cat was out of the bag on that one—finally!), but no one knew about my major health crisis. Once again, I put on the performance of a lifetime, both on air and off. My former drama teachers really deserve kudos!

As news of my impending layoff was playing out in the newspaper, I found I just didn't care anymore. Suddenly, work wasn't important. Station...shmation. Work was suddenly the least of my worries. But you know what? My Girlfriends were there again, as if I'd not just bled them dry with the last emergency (my job). They'd spent months helping me reinvent myself only to send me off to surgery.

My Girlfriend Sue was there for all my appointments, and not just for me, but also for my husband. She took notes because she knew we were all too emotional to remember a dang thing. It was very surreal, almost like watching someone else go through it. Within a month, I'd found out I was definitely losing my job, and now I had a grapefruit-sized tumor. At the very least, I'd have a full and complete hysterectomy if it was benign, and, at the very worst, I had cancer.

The day of my surgery, my husband, mother, and minister were there, along with so many Girlfriends. Jay (my hairdresser) held my mother's hand while my Girlfriend Sue held my husband's. Other Girlfriends kept my children so they wouldn't freak out. They knew Mommy was having surgery, but my Girlfriends kept their schedules fairly normal so Peyton and Marlowe could come through this as unscarred as possible. My kids had already seen me cry about my job and an uncertain future. (I think my daughter's exact words were, "If your job makes you cry so much, why don't you leave?" Ahhh...out of the mouth of babes!) Therefore, we decided there was no need to freak them out about this until we knew what we were dealing with.

In the end, I praise God! The tumor was benign, and I ended up with only a hysterectomy. (By the way, rereading this sentence, I can't believe I just said it was *only* a hysterectomy.) That was the most horrible surgery I could ever imagine. I can only explain that it's like childbirth by C-section with no prize at the end, and you feel like you're strung up inside like a marionette. No matter how you move, it pulls a stitch somewhere that leaves you wanting to strangle the person nearest you! However, the hysterectomy was so much better than the alternative (cancer) that I couldn't have been more relieved!

Relief doesn't mean I was happy about it though. All the morphine in the hospital wasn't enough to cure my blues. I was losing my job, and now all my female parts were gone. What the heck? I'm a good person. Why was this happening to me? That's where my Girlfriends swooped into the hospital room, as if on cue. They made me laugh when I thought laughter was not only improbable, but impossible. For instance, Jay gave me a floral arrangement with a giant bedazzled grapefruit as the center piece. (Get it? A grapefruit size tumor?!) I loved it! Of course, my tumor would have to have some bling! That's just the way I roll...ha!

Then my Girlfriend, Mignon, called me from Kansas and told me I was just like the dang chocolate Easter bunny. Sweet on the outside, but hollow on the inside! There probably couldn't be a better description. Since Todd and I had moved to Tulsa twelve years before, I'd lost my thyroid, gallbladder, and now my female parts. Yep, I am as hollow as the darn chocolate bunny. Oh! How we laughed and laughed at that!

Speaking of laughing...did I mention God has a sense of humor? Because my story isn't over yet....

The day after I returned home after almost a week in the hospital, an Oklahoma storm rolled through (insert Garth Brooks' song "The Thunder Rolls" here). Of course, I was in too much pain to move, but it was fierce outside. Suddenly there was a huge crack (like I'd never heard before!), a scream (my daughter), and a smoky smell (oh, no!). Seriously? Yep, I'm serious. Lightning had struck our freaking house! Somehow I got myself out of bed (anyone who's had a hysterectomy knows that's no small feat) and hobbled outside. I smelled smoke but no fire. Thank God, my home was not on fire. However, once I came back inside I realized that everything from the air conditioning unit to the doorbell was F-R-I-E-D. You heard me right. Our house was about as non-functional on the inside as me! Argh...apparently the chocolate Easter bunny was now living in the dang gingerbread house!

Come on! Three strikes in a little more than a month?! I was losing my job, I had a cancer scare/major surgery, and now our house was struck by lightning! Stick a fork in me...I was done! Read my lips—D-O-N-E! I decided I couldn't take any more. Just give me my morphine and leave me alone! (Yep...time for a pity party!)

About halfway through my third dazed and drugged day back home, I just started laughing hysterically. I'm pretty sure my mother just wrote it off as temporary insanity (which might not be too far off the mark), but actually I couldn't have felt more alive. I'd come to a conclusion that I could just sit around and whine about my job, my health, and my home, or I could change the way I looked at it. From that moment, I decided to think about the last month in a very different way: I had a new and exciting career opportunity, I knew I was cancer free, and our home didn't burn down.

Yes, God does have a sense of humor, and it was time to quit playing the victim and, instead, laugh and deal with it. I immediately called my Original Girlfriend (my mom) into my bedroom and shared my new-found knowledge and wisdom.

That's right. Whether or not you have Girlfriends, there's a point where you have to just suck it up and bring your "A" game! My Girlfriend Sue is a perfect example of that. Two heart attacks and a horse accident later, and she's still so up and positive. Sue knows it and I learned it—your happiness is not up to your Girlfriends or anyone else. It's up to you. If you think your Girlfriends will cure everything this world dishes out, then you're sadly mistaken. They can help you through the hardest times, they can help you overcome, they can help you laugh, but your ultimate happiness is up to you. I have no doubt that when I faced my three strikes in a little more than a month (my livelihood, health, and home), it was a combination of my faith, my outlook, and my Girlfriends that helped me not only survive, but to thrive.

Think about it. For months, I thought losing my job was the worst thing that could happen to me, but I was so wrong. Without my health, I couldn't be the mom and wife I want to be. When our home was threatened, it was just the cherry on top. Material things can be replaced, you can always get a new job, but the health and happiness of your family is the most important thing. Everything is relative, isn't it? And you know what? My family was okay and together regardless of the three strikes. I think I appreciated that more than ever. What a freeing experience. I could gently toss that new Jimmy Choo bag in the closet (with a dust cover on it, of course) without a second thought, as long as I could spend more time with my husband and kids. In fact, I was starting to get excited that when the school year started, I would actually be able to pick my kids up right after school and spend time with them instead of staying at the station until 6:30 at night. Wow! What a concept! I realized everything really would be okay, and we would get through this together.

By the way, you might think my Girlfriends would have been tapped out after months of worrying about my job. But now, beyond my career, my health and home had also been struck (both figuratively and literally). Dang...I might have fired me as a friend! Way too much drama! Instead, my Girlfriends kicked in even more. My "hyster-sisters," Jill and Carmen, made sure I was fed because they'd been there, done that, had bought the t-shirt. Courtney, Marquita, Jennifer, and others took care of my kids while I recuperated, helped my husband get appliances replaced, and still kept me up and positive about my future job opportunities. So many balls in the air and yet they helped me juggle them. Their energy and enthusiasm helped me remain upbeat, focused, and ready for the future.

For the most part, anyway.

I ended up having one last and unexpected meltdown. With only a few weeks left between my surgery and the end of my contract (July 1st, 2009), I wasn't healthy enough to return to work. Somehow it never really occurred to me that I'd already worked my last day and wouldn't be able to say goodbye to my viewers. Hmmm...you might think I would have clued in on that. Not so much. So, on June 31, I decided to get out of bed for an hour and return my new computer that had mysteriously died. (I think that may have been God's way of telling me to take a break from the book and get better...but that's only a hunch.) I moaned and groaned

127

all the way to Best Buy. I stood (painfully!) in line to see a repair technician, only to find out that they would have to replace my entire computer and that I needed to surrender it along with the power cord. Oh yeah...one minor point—that power cord was at home! Leave and do this all over again? No way, mister! So I did what any woman would do who lost her job, had major surgery, had a house struck by lightning, and had been told she couldn't walk out the door with a new computer that minute: I had a total and complete meltdown... right there at the service desk. I'm sure there's surveillance video of that lovely moment somewhere that will come back to haunt me. The more I tried not to cry, the more I broke down. All I could do was hobble over to the chairs usually reserved for bored spouses, whimper as I tried to sit down, and sob into my hand. That poor computer guy wasn't sure what he had done or said, but he looked fairly afraid to ask, fearing more drama. When I could get control enough that I could form part of a sentence, I did the only thing that made sense. I called my Girlfriend Sue.

Now, I can be hormonal with the best of them, but suddenly I could no longer blame that, could I? (Remember...I'm a hyster-sister now.) So, when Sue answered, all I could choke out was "What's. Wrong. With. Me? I. Can't. Get. Control! In. Best. Buy." Without skipping a beat, Sue answered with tremendous wisdom and foresight. "I expected this call today. This would have been your last day at the station."

What...?

It all became clear. My twenty year career (twelve years at the same station) was coming to a close without so much as a party, a goodbye, or a kiss my behind. I had no closure whatsoever.

I wasn't expecting that! I was over it...I was doing good, remember?

Well, maybe not.

Sue came and got me, and we went to (where else?) a bar. Sue decided we would have our own going-away party. (See why I love her?) We had a toast to a job well done as well as a toast to celebrate things to come. (Yes, I was off my morphine at this point, in case you were worried.) We cried, we laughed, and I brushed off my physical and emotional hurt. I wasn't able to last long at the make-shift goodbye party—just long enough to put some issues to bed. Again, one of my board of directors knew just what the doctor ordered.

I did get some closure, though, in mid-July when I was healthy enough to go back to the station and clean out my desk. I can't thank the station enough for that. Almost all the other employees who were laid off were escorted out the door and their desks packed up and sent to them. I appreciate the healing experience of going back to the building to wrap things up. While I didn't get to tell viewers good-bye, at least I got to see all my co-workers one last time.

Now, it was obvious that some people had no idea what to say to me. A couple of people acted like if they talked with me that they too might catch my layoff disease. However, by and large, the friends I'd made over the years at the station hugged me, said they were sorry, and made me feel as if I'd be missed. It certainly wasn't a Girlfriends' sendoff, but it was enough to close out this part of my life with class and dignity. I needed that. To this day, I can thank the station for lifelong Friends like my co-anchor, Mark, and Girlfriend DC. Both of my precious children were born while I worked there, and it was a wonderful place to work. Now it was time to put all my Girlfriends' efforts and life lessons to work and find out about the power of a second chance.

Here's your tenth Girlfriends Challenge:

1. Make sure you have Girlfriends who help you find the bright side and maybe even remind you that laughter is the best medicine.

2. While Girlfriends can help you adjust your attitude and succeed, they are not responsible for it. Ultimately, my dear, that is up to you.

3. If, heaven forbid, you face a few bumps in life's road, just know it is your real Girlfriends who will provide the shock absorbers time and time again.

CHAPTER 11

The power of a second chance.

Once my job and physical healing were officially done, it was time to make some money. You see, with a TV contract, there is no "severance package." When my job was done, so was my income. Again, I thank the station for the heads up in January because all spending at the Morrison household stopped then. (Good thing I bought that Jimmy Chew *before* the bad news, huh?) During the months of limbo, we squirreled away my paycheck, rolled the boat into the mortgage and refinanced, and we paid off any and all credit cards. But now that my income was zip, Todd and I were stressed. Could we live on my husband's salary alone? We could but, like so many families, we'd built our life (and our twenty-year marriage) on dual incomes. We'd certainly learned in 2009 that material things were only, well, material...but that didn't mean we didn't love them!

Fearing the worst, Todd felt obligated to work longer hours so we wouldn't lose what we'd worked so hard to achieve. That was smart and noble, but it wasn't fair. I felt an obligation to my family to try and keep our lifestyle, if possible. (Besides, I wanted to shop at some point again!) If we had to downsize, then so be it. But in the meantime, I was fully prepared to tighten our bootstraps, not touch our savings and do whatever it took to keep our home and, hopefully, Todd's boat.

My book was in the works, and I was beginning to make contacts to hit the national speaking circuit, but those things weren't going to make money for a while. Desperate times call for desperate measures. My first stop was to apply for unemployment. I had finally decided I was not too proud to collect unemployment. I mean, I had been contributing to that fund for twenty years, right? Besides, it was just to help out until something better came along.

The day I applied, I put on a nice suit and my game face, although I noticed my face was a little worse for wear lately. (Stress much?) Luckily, I had a friend who owned a medical spa so I called and asked if I could get a quick Botox refresher. When I worked for the news station, I couldn't accept any freebies because it could give the appearance I'm biased toward a person or company if I ever had to do a report on them. But these days I was not above unemployment *or* favors and, boy, was I in luck. Botox was doing a promotional rebate, and my friend was feeling sorry for me. Fab! I made a quick detour by the spa. That's right, I said it. I'm the only chick you know who gets Botox in the morning and applies for unemployment in the afternoon. Yep, that's how I roll....

By noon, I finally arrived at my original destination feeling younger, chic, and ready to take on the system. However, once I walked in, the lady at the front desk looked at me like I'd grown two heads. Several things went through my mind: Oh, gosh! Is my forehead bruising from the Botox? Or maybe bringing my Jimmy Choo was a bit much when asking for a handout! Then my faux pas came to light. "Honey, you just asked if this is the unemployment office," she said, clearing her throat with disdain. "This is the *employment* office. We help you *find* a job."

Oops.

I mumbled something about this obviously being my first time here, and then proceeded to fill out the paperwork she shoved in my direction. I spent the next few hours updating my employment status on a computer, taking a competency test (yes, I know my right hand from my left), and meeting with a job counselor. By the time I hit the latter, I was spent...especially when she told me my testing showed I was best suited to sell yellow book ads and that she had just the job for me. Huh?

Needless to say, I decided then and there, I would not be on unemployment long! My new business was going to succeed, and I was not going to fall back on unemployment benefits or take another competency test from the federal government. I may not have been in the business school in college, but I knew from that moment that I had the desire to succeed and Girlfriends to help me do it. Mark my words—I do not want to relive that humiliating experience again!

That is when the puzzle pieces began to fall into place.

Within a couple days, I got a call from a Tulsa company that manufactures and sells hearing aids nationwide. They were looking for a new spokesperson and thought I might be a good fit. They had gotten a glowing recommendation from a Friend of mine (thank you, John!). When I met with them, they were incredible. Not only did they like what I suggested for a new marketing campaign, they seemed to think I was pretty good at what I do! (Wow! That's not something you hear often in TV news!) On top of it all, they give

Promotion for Clear-tone along with a pic of SeboTek owners Jim Feeley (left) & Mike Feeley (right)

employees a Bible verse each day and fifteen minutes of quiet time to "start their day off right." I had no idea workplaces like that existed! In a newsroom, the only moment of silence is when someone shouted a cuss word only to discover the local cub scouts are there taking a tour! I was in heaven and thrilled when we signed a deal. While my last situation with Corporate America made me feel like a lamb chop, SeboTek (which owns Clear-tone) restored my faith in big business.

Next, I got my first national speaking gig right in Tulsa! Jeff Magee (my speaking buddy) brought together some of the area's top speakers to do an all-day seminar called "Get Real" to motivate local business leaders. I was thrilled to be on the agenda. Even better? My Girlfriends showed up en masse. Sure, there were a lot of business folks and entrepreneurs, but there were just as many of my Girlfriends who either signed up to attend for the day or crowded into the back to cheer me on: Melanie, Deedra, Heidi, JoAnna, Michelle, Chris, Rick, Cindy, my husband...the list goes on and on. I was almost moved to tears when I hit the stage. They all knew this was a big step toward my dream, and they wanted to share it.

Jeff Magee, Billy Joe Daugherty, Me & Michael Butler @ speaking event

In fact, two of my Girlfriends who were there— Deedrea and Melanie—are also former news gals who are doing their own entrepreneurial thing. They started a website called 918Moms.com, which had grown by leaps and bounds, and was about to be bought out by a media outlet. Just days earlier, we had met at our favorite restaurant to talk about our latest successes. When I arrived, the Girls were there waiting with champagne to literally toast our new lives (sniff!). Those are the kinds of

Just a few of my Girlfriends who showed up to hear my first national speaking gig

918 Moms Toast to success w/ Melanie (left) & Deerdra (right)

135

Girlfriends who showed up at my big debut. There was neither a Suzie Sabotage nor Helen Hater to be found, just my Support Network. That's exactly what I spoke about that day—why your support system can help you succeed or fail in business. (Me... talking about business...who knew?)

When I finished speaking, each of my Girlfriends hugged me, except for one. The one who hung back and waited until the end? My husband. Once everyone else was done, Todd held me tight, and with an emotional crack in his voice, he managed to choke out only five words. "I'm so proud of you." My heart just swells when I think back to that moment. This was a man who never once questioned, since January, what I was doing or the fact that there were no salary guarantees. Instead, he let me dream and he believed in me.

w/ Todd (my Rock)

In fact, I'm not sure I've given him enough credit in this book. He's a huge part of why my Girlfriend Support Network works, because he is my best Friend (with benefits, of course!). Maybe that's why Todd doesn't second guess why I need advice from the Girls, and he's not threatened by the Guyfriends who add value to my life. Without Todd and his support, I'm not sure I could have taken such big risks. I know it sounds sappy, but it's true. I think I picked my husband the way I pick my Girlfriends—a "10" who supports me and makes me a better person. Thank you, Pookie!

After that day, other things began to fall into place. While many people kept telling me "Girlfriend topics won't make you any money," gigs kept rolling in. By September, I had been asked to join a select group of women hosting a show on a new Internet site called The WIN—Women's Information Network. The hosts all converged on Salt Lake City to meet, greet, and make the site a reality. Oh, my! I don't think I've ever been in a room with that many powerful and savvy women. Some of the top speakers and women entrepreneurs in the country were there! While we networked and helped each other during the day (well, they helped me)...it was a big slumber party at night. That trip sealed the deal that I was doing the right thing. Women empowering women is huge! And if I could be a part of that, I would be blessed...and lucky.

In fact, I made such good Girlfriends there that one of them, Kellee, a big women's magazine editor, flew me to California to help her with the huge women's conference there. While working her booth, we also hobnobbed with wonderful women like Robin Roberts from "Good

Kellee from Women of Wisdom Magazine

Morning America," Olympian Dara Torres and Brenda Strong from the TV Show "Desperate Housewives." I can only describe it as the ultimate Girlfriend experience. Like Salt Lake City, it combined a Girlfriends' vacay with wonderful advice and enrichment.

My, how much my life has changed in just one year. Back in January 2009, I thought I was a one-trick pony. I knew nothing about business and although I was confident in front of a camera or an audience, I'm not sure I totally believed in myself. Isn't that ironic? Speaking of irony, by January 2010, businesses started lining up to call me for consultations and to speak to their employees about doing their job better. And hey, I didn't even have to go back to school and study business! Nope. Instead, I had my Girlfriends, who not only taught me the basics and pulled the businesswoman from the depths of my soul (who knew?), they helped me through the dark times when I was only held together with twine on the inside. Financially, physically, and emotionally, my Girlfriends made me a better woman. While they've been there all my life, they were really there when the chips were down.

But, boy, sometimes it's hard to teach a mid-life dog new tricks. Toward the end of 2009, my Guyfriend David (a Fringe Friend who became a spiritual mentor to me) asked, "Cindy, you used to be in TV. Who are you today?" I proudly said, "I'm an Emmy-winning journalist who's an author, speaker, consultant, and mom." He stunned me when he said, "Cindy, you're just replacing one title with another. That's what you do...that's not who you are." Wow...was he right. I guess I wanted so desperately to be somebody the last twenty years that I still hadn't totally gotten it through my thick skull that my identity is not my job. As I mentioned before, society is quick to put you in a labeled box identified by what you "do." I'd bought into that hook, line and sinker. So, who am I *today*? Hmmm...I'm a mom who picked my kids up in the after-school pickup line this year for the first time ever. I'm a caretaker who didn't have to worry about

Todd has been there through thick & thin.

My Friends have always been there...win or lose.

I'm so proud to be a mommy!

I feel truly blessed.

I value my Girlfriends & their never ending support.

I owe my Girlfriends so much!

I can't thank my parents enough.

My Girlfriends ROCK.

Family comes first.

what my boss would think when my kids got the swine flu. I'm a wife who got more than my money's worth when I met my future husband at Penny Beer Night more than twenty years ago. I'm a daughter who thinks my parents hung the moon, and I can't imagine life without them. And I'm a Girlfriend who has been blessed with wonderful Friends who have been bridesmaids, fashion editors, life coaches, and business professors. It's your you-ness that makes you somebody and who you choose to surround yourself with...not a title, a job, or money.

The night before my book was due to the publisher, my Girlfriends 2.0 philosophy came full circle. You see, a month before, one of my dear sweet Girlfriends died of breast cancer. MaryAnn was one of the sweetest people you could possibly know. Not only was she a Girlfriend's Girlfriend, her smile could light up a room, and she laughed from her head to her toes. Amazingly, she met the love of her life, Rick, just three years ago. The cancer diagnosis was devastating. Not only was there a chance she could leave this earth too soon, she couldn't bear the thought of leaving her soul-mate even one moment too early. Unfortunately, the cancer finally won. She will be missed....

One night in December, all of MaryAnn's Girlfriends had a date to decorate for Christmas. MaryAnn loved the season, and we knew she wouldn't want Rick to be alone or not celebrate the holiday. We showed up and went to work. Halfway through, we all sat around the table and ate dinner. We raised a toast, we cried, we laughed. It's what Girlfriends do. We take care of our own, no matter the circumstances. Yes, we're all busy, but when it counts, we're there for each other and our loved ones. As I looked around at these precious Girlfriends, I knew this was the ending of my book.

I've said it before and I'll say it again: You can't pick your parents, and you may or may not have picked a good spouse. But each and every one of us can pick wonderful Girlfriends to enrich our lives, pick us up when we're down, and make our world a better place—even after we leave this earth. I challenge you to not define yourself by your job or by material things, but instead define yourself by who you really are and with whom you surround yourself. If your Girlfriends aren't making you the best person you can be, it's time to reboot and upgrade. Remember, whether you need to leave the flock and jump a fence to freedom, reinvent yourself, survive a divorce, kick a bad habit, or simply remind yourself of the Christmas spirit, your Girlfriends are there for you....

Always.

Now, go spread the love!

W/ Girlfriend Stephanie and precious MaryAnn

Your final Girlfriends Challenge:

Put your Girlfriends on your "To Do" list.

1. Text, Tweet or Facebook your Girlfriends at least once a week.

2. Call your long-distance Girlfriends at least once a month.

3. Have a Girl's Night out once a month or so to follow up, support one another, and to simply reconnect.

The Ten Keys to Having Lifelong Girlfriends

How do you truly build a cache of wonderful, lifelong Girlfriends? You just need to allow caring people into your life who only want the best for you, and you must dump the wanna-bes. You know who I'm talking about. They're the people who "wanna be" your friend, but either never learned how or simply can't be a good friend for whatever reason. These emotional vampires will suck you dry and have no place in your life.

So how do you find the "right" Girlfriends? I believe a Girlfriend is a learned and earned position. That's right. You don't start off being a great friend from the moment you're born, but instead you learn how to be a truly good Friend over time. It's also a position you earn. I sat down with some of my best Girlfriends who have earned my complete trust to decide what exactly makes some Girlfriends keepers, and some girlfriends (notice no capitalization) only wanna-bes.

1 No hidden agenda.

My Girlfriend Sue had reminded me of this one for years! Someone really isn't a friend if she tries to get close to you because of your job, your money, or something else she thinks is important. I have to tell you, I learned who my real friends were after I got laid off from my very public job as a local newscaster. My real Girlfriends stuck by me, helped me pick up the pieces, and gave me the strength to put my life back together again. There's nothing glamorous about that! Agendas come and go, but real friends are there through thick and thin, fat and skinny, or rich and poor.

#2 Your true Girlfriends are supportive emotionally and physically.

These are the Girlfriends who will give you a hug when you need one, they always have a shoulder for you to cry on, and they have a high-five ready and waiting when you succeed.

#3 Your friends are not afraid to be gently honest. (This is a biggie!)

All four of us agreed that honesty is key, but here's where the "gently" comes in. If my husband tells me my pants aren't flattering? Well, that might come with strings attached. (Did he just say I'm fat?) So he ends up sleeping in the guestroom for a week. But my Girlfriends will usually say something like, "Hmmm...I'm not sure that's the best look." No feelings are hurt and I look my best. Just remember, be gentle with your honesty.

#4 You're not guarded with your real Girlfriend.

We all got quite a kick out of this one, but it's true. When you're with your real Girlfriends, you don't always feel like you have to edit what you say. You can speak your mind, and you don't have to worry all the time you might offend someone. Besides if you do, they'll be "gently honest" about it and then forgive you.

#5 Really good Girlfriends can agree to disagree.

Just because you're best buddies doesn't mean you agree on everything, from politics to religion. My Girlfriend Sue and I respect each other enough that we have agreed to disagree on many a topic.

#6 Friendship is not a competition! Never ever!

My Girlfriend Heidi is a model, and yet I'm not jealous of her. In fact, I take great pride in her accomplishments and I'm thrilled I get to share those moments with a woman who has a heart of gold and is a wonderful Friend. My Girlfriend group is one that celebrates successes and toasts achievements. The legendary Zig Ziglar may have said it best: "You will have everything in life you want...if you will help other people get what they want." If someone is jealous or looks at your friendship as a competition...forget it.

#7 No guilt.

Everyone is busy and it's hard to get together, but when you do? It should be like no time has passed. Every year, two of my Girlfriends and I take a girls' vacay and catch up. We all live in different states and talk by phone and email...but still, we have eight kids between us all! When we finally have time to get away from it all and catch up, there's no guilt that time has passed. Instead, we pick right up where we left off.

145

#8 There's no tit-for-tat in a true friendship.

We're not keeping score of how many times my child spends the night or you pick up the kids after school. We just do what we can do, help each other, and realize that it all balances out in the end.

#9 You always share your best secrets.

This is one of my favorites! Knowledge is not power in a Friendship. Instead, true Friendship is a shared experience. Whether you've just found the best mascara on the face of the planet or the secret to potty training, you always share the wealth with your sistas!

#10 When you can't laugh, your Girlfriends make you laugh anyway.

This is a must! No one can make me laugh in the face of trouble faster than my Girlfriends. When I got laid off, had a hysterectomy, and my house got struck by lightning in a little more than a month, it was my Girlfriends who reminded me that God has a sense of humor. Your Girlfriends can always help you find the bright side and maybe even remind you that laughter is the best medicine.

Emmy-winning TV broadcaster **Cindy Morrison** successfully reinvented herself after the economy lead to corporate downsizing and left her unemployed. Leaving her 20-year career behind, Morrison wrote "Girlfriends 2.0" to empower women to upgrade their Girlfriend Network. She has since been speaking on the topic and has launched a successful consulting business, Reinvention 2.0, a business-focused approach to her Girlfriends 2.0 concept. Morrison's

The Morrison Family
(Courtesy Jill Solomon
Photography)

witty and approachable speaking style was honed during her many years as a television news anchor and investigative reporter in Tulsa and Oklahoma City, OK. She has won an Emmy, a Peabody, and a Gracie Allen Award for her groundbreaking investigations over the years. Morrison also hosts national shows for the Woman's Information Network and the Diva Toolbox. In 2010, she was chosen as one of the 25 Most Amazing Women of the Year by Stiletto Women Magazine. She is also a member of the National Speaker's Association and continues her loyal membership with numerous other national news organizations.

Along with her "Girlfriends 2.0" book, Cindy hosts a popular show by the same name for the Women's Information Network (The WIN). The idea is to empower women so they can not only survive but thrive our changing times. She also speaks across the country about "Reinvention 2.0" and how anyone can network strategically to be more successful. As a consultant, Cindy's clients range from TV stations to major universities to heavy hitting corporations. On top of all that, Cindy is also the national spokesperson for the Tulsa based company Clear-tone.

Cindy spent a dozen years as a nightly news anchor and lead investigative reporter in Tulsa, OK. Prior to that, Cindy also spent nearly a decade as an anchor and reporter in Oklahoma City. The veteran journalist won an Emmy, Peabody and Gracie Allen Award for her ground breaking investigation and has covered such major stories as the OKC bombing and the 51-day cult standoff in Waco, Texas for stations across the country including Good Morning America.

Bring Cindy Morrison's teachings to life!

Cindy shows people how to reboot, upgrade and reinvent through networking, social media and branding so they can make more money and live a better life.

Girlfriends 2.0
How would you like to immediately spot Suzie Sabotage? Surround yourself with supportive Girlfriends? And build a life balance so you can thrive? Cindy is available for speaking engagements, breakout sessions and book signings about how to reboot and upgrade YOUR Girlfriend Network so you can not only survive but thrive!

Reinvention 2.0
How would you like to reinvent yourself to make more money? Create brand loyalty for free? Become prime time ready overnight? Cindy offers speaking engagements and breakout sessions about reinventing yourself so you can turn your passion into dollars. It's how to get the kind of publicity money can't buy. This is a must for men and women in our changing economic times.

For Bookings: Booking@CindyWMorrison.com